# Ten Parts in the King
## The Prophesied Reconciliation
## of
## God's Two Witnesses

### PETER G. RAMBO, SR.

Ten Parts in the King, by Peter G. Rambo, Sr.
Published by Kindle Direct Publishing

tenpartsintheking.com

Copyright © 2018 Peter G. Rambo, Sr.

All rights reserved. No portion of this book may be reproduced in any form without permission from the author, except as permitted by U.S. copyright law. For permissions contact: editor@tenpartsintheking.com

Cover by Ralphie Cratty

Illustrations on pages 4, 43, 56, 74, 108, 124, 146, and 172 are taken from eBooks in the public domain available at Project Gutenberg, www.gutenberg.org.

ISBN: 9781729385678

Scripture quotations taken from the New American Standard Bible® (NASB), Copyright © 1960, 1962, 1963, 1968, 1971, 1972, 1973, 1975, 1977, 1995 by The Lockman Foundation. Used by permission. www.Lockman.org

DEDICATION

*To the memory of Keith Gordon Green*
*October 21, 1953 – July 28, 1982*
*The seeds sown in a life so short still bear fruit a lifetime later.*

# CONTENTS

| | | |
|---|---|---|
| | List of Maps and Illustrations | vi |
| | Acknowledgments | viii |
| | Glossary | xi |
| | Introduction: Pictured in a Parable | 1 |
| 1 | When God Divides the House | 5 |
| 2 | The Ten Tribes and the Two Tribes | 19 |
| 3 | House of Israel ≠ House of Judah | 35 |
| 4 | A Tale of Twos | 44 |
| 5 | The Rabbis Were Right | 57 |
| 6 | One Kingdom, Two Destinies | 75 |
| 7 | Apostolic Expectations, Part 1:<br>A Message for Two Brothers | 92 |
| 8 | Apostolic Expectations, Part 2:<br>The Gospel of the Kingdom | 110 |
| 9 | Finding Israelite Identity in the New Covenant | 127 |
| 10 | One Seed | 150 |
| 11 | Frequently Asked Questions | 162 |
| 12 | Implications and Conclusions | 177 |

## MAPS AND ILLUSTRATIONS

| | |
|---|---|
| How many "Houses" are there in Israel? | 4 |
| Jacob's Twelve Sons | 18 |
| Israel's Two Houses | 34 |
| Tribal Allotments After the Conquest of Canaan | 43 |
| An Ancient Near East Superpower | 56 |
| Division of the Kingdom | 74 |
| Two Angry Brothers, Part 1: Levi | 91 |
| Two Angry Brothers, Part 2: Simeon | 109 |
| The Case Against Dan | 126 |
| Manasseh's Double Portion | 149 |
| Benjamin's Special Role | 161 |
| The Tribes and the Throne of God | 176 |

# ACKNOWLEDGMENTS

Radical shifts in thought do not happen in a vacuum. Rather, they occur after a significant amount of data is collected and processed, forcing a conclusion that sets a new course. Such was the case when Copernicus and Galileo dared to propose that the sun, rather than the earth, is at the center of our part of the galaxy. They did not reach their conclusions in day, but through of lifetime of study that built on the work of others who had gone before them.

The book you hold in your hands is the culmination of processing through the influences and challenges presented by the voices of many men and women from the present and past. The studied eye perusing these acknowledgments will find a list of people who love and affirm the God of Abraham, Isaac, and Jacob, yet seemingly stand at odds with each other. In fact, I believe many on this list would be very uncomfortable being in the same room with others listed. This grieves me. As you read this book, you will understand why.

Everyone on this list worships the God of Israel, and all desire to see Messiah come in power and glory. What has divided them is not the expectant hope of the Messianic Kingdom, but their different views of what this coming King and Kingdom will look like. What we have all failed to recognize, and part of what this book will reveal, is that we all play for the same team and have the same goal.

The goal of a football team is to win each game, and ultimately bring home a championship. Yet the team is diverse, consisting of squads designed for offense, defense, and special teams, with many specialized skill sets required for each position. So, too, is the team God has assembled to compete for the restoration of all Creation. The common failing of the players on God's team is that we often mistake our true opponent: instead of working together to overcome the adversary who hinders the restoration of Creation, we compete against each other.

Lumbering offensive tackles do not make fleet-footed cornerbacks, and beefy centers do not make slippery kickoff return men. Nevertheless, each can appreciate the contribution the others provide to the team, and can rejoice in their success on the field of play. In like manner, as this book will reveal, all of us – Christian, Jewish (Messianic and non-Messianic), and Hebrew Roots – have specialized roles and responsibilities in the restoration of the tent of David and the reconciliation of all things. Sadly, what we tend to do is cast obstacles in each other's path rather than cheer each other on.

There is not enough space here to list all the sages, both Christian and Jewish, and the many others who brought us to this point. I regret that I cannot name everyone who has affected my growth and thought processes, but these are the major influencers who have led and taught, or challenged me, such that I was forced to dig deeper into scripture for solutions to perplexing problems. My mention of them does not mean they agree with the message of this book, nor that I agree with everything they have written and taught. What it means is that I am attempting to render proper honor to those who deserve it, regardless of our differences.

I have chosen to list alphabetically. Thank you Abba that You, O Holy One, love us all and desire that we come together in peace and unity.

Thanks and special acknowledgements to:

| | |
|---|---|
| Rivkah Lambert Adler | Toby Janicki |
| Holissa Alewine | Rick Joyner |
| Ovadyah Avrahami | Monte Judah |
| Zach Bauer | Dan Juster |
| Adam Eliyahu Berkowitz | Lane Keister |
| Bill Bright | Moshe Kempinski |
| Michael Brown | D. Thomas Lancaster |
| Eddie Chumney | C. S. Lewis |
| Mikell Clayton | Josh McDowell |
| Bill Cloud | J.K. McKee |
| Steven M. Collins | Boaz Michael |
| Rico Cortes | Steve Moutria |
| Margot Crossing | James Pyle |

| | |
|---|---|
| Yair Davidiy | Pamela Fellers Rambo |
| Charity Dell | Ken Rank |
| David Fohrman | James I. Riley, Jr. |
| Ephraim & Rimona Frank | Michael Rood |
| Chaim Goldman | Brad Scott |
| Joseph Goode | Itzhak Shapira |
| Nehemia Gordon | Jon Sherman |
| Tim Hegg | R.C. Sproul |
| Daniel Holdings | Peter Vest |
| Mark Huey | Batya & Angus Wootten |
| Asher Intrater | Hanoch Young |

Many thanks to the professors of Columbia Biblical Seminary, Columbia International University – especially Igou Hodges and William Larkin.

I owe a debt of gratitude to current and former Elders of B'ney Yosef North America for their guidance, wise counsel, and friendship. This book would not have been possible without their input in more ways than they probably recognize – Ed Boring, John Conrad, Frank Houtz, David E. Jones, Johnny Marrs, Barry Phillips, David Sloss, Iglahliq Suuqiina, and Mark Webb.

As very special personal acknowledgement, I wish to recognize and thank my bride, Kelly C. Rambo, for her patience and support. Others who merit special recognition and thanks, particularly for their editing skills, listening ear, prayers, and general feedback as this book was shaped, are Anisa Baker, Ed Boring, Cathy Helms, Tommy and Dorothy Wilson, and especially, Ephraim and Rimona Frank.

May Abba bless each of these and those we may have overlooked for their dedicated Kingdom service.

# GLOSSARY

This is not a comprehensive list of the terms used in this book, but rather a quick reference guide to the most important terms which might be new to a reader unfamiliar with the Torah Awakening and the biblical history of the nation of Israel.

**Apostolic Writings.** The New Testament, also known as the Brit Chadashah (New Covenant). I regard these 27 books (Matthew through Revelation) as part of the revealed Word of God on the same authoritative level as the entire Tanakh (Old Testament).

**Appointed Times.** See Feasts of the Lord.

**Ephraim.** The younger son of Joseph who, together with his brother Manasseh, was adopted by his grandfather Jacob and given status as head of a tribe and bearer of the family name of Israel (Genesis 48:8-22). Ephraim became the chief tribe of the House of Joseph and leader of the Ten Tribes of Israel's Northern Kingdom.

**Ephraimite.** Biblically, a member of the tribe of Ephraim. Today, Ephraimites are those who identify as Hebrews and Israelites of the House of Joseph/Ephraim.

**Feasts of the Lord.** The Appointed Times of God as explained in Leviticus 23. These are: the weekly Sabbath (*Shabbat*), Passover (*Pesach*), Unleavened Bread (*Matzot*), First Fruits (*Yom Habikkurim*), Pentecost (*Shavuot*), Trumpets (*Yom Teruah*, *Rosh Hashanah*), Atonement (*Yom Kippur*), and Tabernacles (*Sukkot*). The Hebrew term for these special times is *moed* (plural, *moedim*) (מוֹעֵד, Strongs #H4150).

**Hebraic/Hebrew Roots Believer.** A person who believes Yeshua (Jesus) is the Messiah, honors the Torah, and identifies as a Hebrew (member of the nation of Israel). This term generally applies to non-Jewish persons holdings these beliefs, particularly to those who accept the tenets of Two House theology.

**Hebrew.** The name applied to Abraham and his descendants who became the nation of Israel (Genesis 14:3, 39:13-18, 43:32; Exodus 1:15-19). It comes from the name of Abraham's ancestor Eber (Genesis 11:16), and equates to the word *ivriy* (עִבְרִי, Strongs #H5680). I use the term to refer not only to the Jewish descendants of Abraham, but to those who identify as Hebrews of the non-Jewish House of Joseph/Ephraim.

**House of David.** The ruling dynasty of the united kingdom of Israel, founded by King David (2 Samuel 7:8-29).

**House of Joseph.** Refers both to the tribes founded by Joseph's two sons, Ephraim and Manasseh, and to the non-Jewish tribes that allied with them when the united kingdom of Israel was divided (the "Lost Ten Tribes"). Also known as the House of Israel, and as Ephraim (Joshua 17:17-18, Ezekiel 37:15-19).

**House of Judah.** The Jewish part of Israel, named for the tribe of Judah. When Israel was divided, the tribes of Judah, Benjamin, and most of Levi formed Israel's Southern Kingdom, known as Judah. The Jewish people today are descended from the House of Judah (2 Samuel 2:5-11, 1 Kings 12:20-21).

**Israel.** The Covenant Nation of YHVH, established by the patriarchs Abraham, Isaac, and Jacob. Israel consists both of the Jewish House of Judah, and the non-Jewish House of Israel (also known as Joseph and Ephraim).

**Lost Ten Tribes.** The tribes of the Northern Kingdom of Israel, known also as Joseph, and as Ephraim. These tribes rebelled against the House of David, united under the leadership of Ephraim, and eventually were conquered by the Assyrian Empire. The Lost Tribes have been scattered to every part of the world, and now are mixed with every nation and people. The redemption and restoration of the Lost Tribes, and their reunion with Judah, is the a major theme of biblical prophecy, and is tied directly to the work of the Messiah.

**Messiah.** The savior, redeemer, and future ruler of Israel and the world. "Messiah" comes from the Hebrew *mashiach*, or "anointed one." This Hebrew term is equivalent to the Greek term *christos*, from which we get the English word Christ.

**Messianic.** A person who believes Yeshua (Jesus) is the Messiah, and who also believes the Torah is applicable to Yeshua's followers. Our use of the term generally applies to Messianic Jews rather than to non-Jewish followers of Yeshua who honor the Torah.

**Moedim.** See Feasts of the Lord

**Talmud.** The compilation of Jewish law and commentary on scripture. It consists of two parts: the Mishnah, which is a systematic codification of rabbinic law (the "Oral Law"), and the Gemara, which are rabbinic commentaries on the Mishnah. Mainstream Judaism regards the Mishnah as scripture and the authoritative Word of God. Christianity has never considered the Mishnah as scripture. Much of the Messianic/Hebrew Roots community regard the Mishnah and Gemara as very important and instructive writings, but agrees with Christianity that they are not on the same level as scripture.

**Tanakh.** The Old Testament, consisting of the Torah (Five Books of Moses), Nevi'im (Prophets), and Ketuvim (Writings). The word is actually a Hebrew acronym of the first letters of these three sections: T-N-K. The Tanakh consists of the 39 books from Genesis to Malachi (according to the Christian arrangement of the canon; the Jewish order is slightly different). I regard each of these books as part of the revealed Word of God, and therefore the highest level of authority.

**Torah.** The Law, Teaching, and Commandments of God, often called simply the Law, or the Law of Moses. I define the Torah as the five books of Moses (Genesis, Exodus, Leviticus, Numbers, Deuteronomy). As scripture, these books are the Word of God and applicable to all of God's people. In this I agree with Judaism, but I disagree regarding the Mishnah (Oral Law), which mainstream Judaism regards as part of the Torah and therefore also the revealed Word of God. I respect the Mishna and the rest of the Talmud as valuable instruction, but I do not consider it authoritative scripture on the same level as the five books of Moses.

**Torah Observant.** The practice of keeping (honoring, observing, obeying), the Torah as commanded by God through Moses. Christians already keep much of the Torah, although they are not aware that they do. As Yeshua said, the weightier provisions of the Law are justice, mercy, and faithfulness (Matthew 23:23; see also Micah 6:8 and Deuteronomy 10:12-13). He also identified the two greatest commandments as loving God and loving others (Mark 12:28-31; see also Deuteronomy 6:4-5 and Leviticus 19:18). What Christians generally do not do is keep the Sabbath on the seventh day (Saturday), celebrate the Feasts of the Lord (Passover, Pentecost, Tabernacles, etc.), eat a biblically clean diet per Leviticus 11, or wear *tzitzit* (tassels) on their garments to remind them of God's commandments (Numbers 15:37-41). These are the major provisions of Torah which Jews and Messianic/Hebraic followers of Yeshua honor, but which most of Christianity does not.

**Torah Awakening.** The global phenomenon among Christians (and others) who are coming to understand that the Torah is applicable not only to Jews, but to all people (Isaiah 2:2-4, 24:3-6, 56:1-7). This awakening has led many people to a process of Torah observance, and often to an understanding of their own Israelite identity.

**Two Houses.** Judah and Joseph (also known as Ephraim), the two major divisions of the nation of Israel. Judah is the Jewish people; Joseph/Ephraim is the non-Jewish portion of Israel, consisting of the Ten Tribes of the Northern Kingdom which were conquered by the Assyrian Empire, scattered throughout the world, and lost their identity.

**Yeshua.** The Hebrew name transliterated in English as Jesus. Messiah Yeshua is the same person as Jesus Christ.

**YHVH.** The Name of God, transliterated from the Hebrew יהוה. There is no consensus on pronunciation of the Divine Name, which is why I choose only to present it as these four letters (the *Tetragrammaton*).

# INTRODUCTION

# PICTURED IN A PARABLE

There is an account in the scriptures that presents a prophetic picture of the coming Messianic age. It concerns the aftermath of the civil war in Israel that erupted when Absalom usurped the throne from his father David (2 Samuel 15-18). When David's loyal forces had defeated the rebels in battle on the eastern side of the Jordan River, the king prepared to return across the river to regain his throne in Jerusalem. This is where we find a peculiar turn of events:

> Then King David sent to Zadok and Abiathar the priests, saying, "Speak to the elders of Judah, saying, 'Why are you the last to bring the king back to his house, since the word of all Israel has come to the king, *even* to his house? You are my brothers; you are my bone and my flesh. Why then should you be the last to bring back the king?' Say to Amasa, 'Are you not my bone and my flesh? May God do so to me, and more also, if you will not be commander of the army before me continually in place of Joab.'" Thus he turned the hearts of all the men of Judah as one man, so that they sent *word* to the king, *saying*, "Return, you and all your servants." The king then returned and came as far as the Jordan. And Judah came to Gilgal in order to go to meet the king, to bring the king across the Jordan. (2 Samuel 19:11-15)[1]

Why would Judah not reclaim their king? Perhaps because the rebellion against him originated from within Judah; when Absalom

---

[1] Unless otherwise specified, scripture quotations are taken from the New American Standard Bible® (NASB), Copyright © 1960, 1962, 1963, 1968, 1971, 1972, 1973, 1975, 1977, 1995 by The Lockman Foundation. Used by permission. www.Lockman.org.

claimed the throne, he did so from Hebron, the city of Judah where David first reigned over his own tribe and House (2 Samuel 5:4-5, 15:7-12). Doubtless there was a large degree of shame involved, particularly on the part of Amasa, the Judean commander of Absalom's army. Nevertheless, the king would not return until his own kin acknowledged him and welcomed him back – something which another son of David said many centuries later:

> Jerusalem, Jerusalem, who kills the prophets and stones those who are sent to her! How often I wanted to gather your children together, the way a hen gathers her chicks under her wings, and you were unwilling. Behold, your house is being left to you desolate! For I say to you, from now on you will not see Me until you say, "BLESSED IS HE WHO COMES IN THE NAME OF THE LORD!"[2] (Matthew 23:37-39)

Today, the Christian world acknowledges Yeshua Son of David as Messiah and King of Israel, but oddly enough does not acknowledge their own part in that same Kingdom. Jews, for the most part, do not acknowledge Yeshua as anyone of importance to them (other than inspiring centuries of virulent anti-Semitism), but they jealously guard the nation of Israel and their place within it. That, too, is reminiscent of the aftermath of Absalom's rebellion:

> Now the king went on to Gilgal, and Chimham went on with him; and all the people of Judah and also half the people of Israel accompanied the king. And behold, all the men of Israel came to the king and said to the king, "Why had our brothers the men of Judah stolen you away, and brought the king and his household and all David's men with him over the Jordan?" Then all the men of Judah answered the men of Israel, "Because the king is a close relative to us. Why then are you angry about this matter? Have we eaten at all at the

---

[2] The first-century apostles quoted extensively from the Old Testament (known in Hebrew as the Tanakh) in their writings. That should not be a surprise since the "Old Testament" was the only portion of Scripture in existence at the time. The New American Standard Bible is very helpful in identifying these extensive quotations. They appear in capital letters with marginal notes citing the reference. For example, in this passage from Matthew 23, the phrase, "BLESSED IS HE WHO COMES IN THE NAME OF THE LORD," is taken from Psalm 118:26.

king's *expense*, or has anything been taken for us?" **But the men of Israel answered the men of Judah and said, "We have ten parts in the king, therefore we also have more *claim* on David than you. Why then did you treat us with contempt? Was it not our advice first to bring back our king?"** Yet the words of the men of Judah were harsher than the words of the men of Israel. (2 Samuel 19:40-43, emphasis added)

The Ten Tribes today are becoming aware of their identity. That is the fruit of the worldwide Torah Awakening sweeping through Christianity. As Christians awaken to the fact that the Torah (the Law, Teaching, and Commandments of God, often called simply the Law) is still applicable today, they also are awakening to the fact that they are part of the nation of Israel. Unlike Jews, who can trace their ancestry to the ancient House of Judah, these awakening Hebrews are known as *Ephraimites*, a people linked through time and spirit to the ancient non-Jewish part of God's Covenant Nation known in scripture by the names House of Israel, House of Joseph, and House of Ephraim.

These newly-aware Hebrews are beginning to look to their brethren of Judah and say, *"We have ten parts in the king."* Some, like our ancestors, continue to say, "Therefore we also have more claim on David than you." They do not speak for all of us. A growing number of modern-day Ephraimites have recognized that our return to full fellowship with our King means a return in humility to reconcile with the Jewish brethren we have envied all these centuries, and who have suffered immeasurably from the fruit of our envy.

If the testimony of scripture is true, then there are two parts to the nation of Israel – two Houses, each with a distinct mission, but together destined to complete a single, united Kingdom in the age of Messiah's reign from Zion.

My purpose is not to convince, but to present the evidence.

I invite you to weigh the evidence for yourself to discern if these things are true.

## How Many "Houses" Are There in Israel?

"House" in this sense is not a building where a family lives, but a *household*. It refers to an extended family, including ancestors and descendants, both native born and attached (such as servants). Israel contains many houses.

Gustave Doré, "Joseph Making Himself Known to His Brethren," in *The Doré Bible Gallery*, (Chicago: Belford-Clarke Co. Publishers, 1891).

HOUSE OF JACOB: All of Israel. The nation gained its name from the patriarch Jacob, whom God renamed Israel upon his return to the Promised Land (Genesis 32:24-32).

HOUSE OF DAVID: Israel's ruling dynasty, from which Messiah comes. King David came from the tribe of Judah, and ruled over the House of Judah before becoming king of the united nation. After the rebellion of the northern tribes, David's descendants retained their position as rulers of Judah. (1 Samuel 20:16, 2 Samuel 2:11, 7:25-27, Zechariah 12:7-10).

HOUSE OF JUDAH: The tribe of Judah, and the southern kingdom of Israel (1 Kings 12:21-24, Hosea 1:7).

HOUSE OF ISRAEL: Sometimes this refers to the entire nation of Israel, but usually it refers to the northern tribes who established a separate kingdom in rebellion against the House of David (1 Kings 12:16-19, Hosea 1:4).

HOUSE OF JOSEPH: Jacob's son Joseph fathered two of Israel's tribes: Ephraim and Manasseh (Genesis 48:8-22). This term refers to those tribes (Joshua 17:17), as well as the northern House of Israel (2 Samuel 19:16-23, 1 Kings 11:26-40, Obadiah 1:18).

HOUSE OF EPHRAIM: Joseph's second son Ephraim inherited the family name when his grandfather Jacob passed the birthright to him (Genesis 48:8-22). House of Ephraim refers not only to the tribe he fathered, but to the entire northern House of Israel, of which Ephraim was the chief tribe (Isaiah 7:17, Hosea 6:10).

# 1

# WHEN GOD DIVIDES THE HOUSE

One of my earliest memories of television was watching the Clemson Tigers defeat the powerful Nebraska Cornhusker football team in the 1981 Orange Bowl for the coveted National Championship. My grandfather was a 1940 graduate of Clemson and a rabid fan of his alma mater. He had season tickets to the football games, and I remember many balmy Saturday afternoons tailgating, grilling and throwing a football around in addition to climbing high in the Death Valley stadium to watch another match on the gridiron. Most fall weekends were planned around either attending the games or listening on the radio or watching the television our my beloved Tigers clawed for victory.

How could I not grow up a devoted fan? Everyone in my family was a Clemson fan. Well, almost everyone. My brother, Jonathan, 'converted' to the "dark side" and is a vocal South Carolina Gamecocks fan. The University of South Carolina has long been Clemson's hated in-state rival. In the early 1900's the rivalry was so fierce at one point that knives and guns were involved in a showdown between fans.

Collegiate football in the South is a religion. Everything through the week, from water cooler conversation at work to party planning, revolves around Saturday's games. Every major team has an archrival that fuels competitive jabs and sometimes grave division. Clemson has South Carolina, Florida State has Florida, Alabama has Auburn, Georgia has Georgia Tech, and the list goes on. Many, many rivalries span generations with rabid fans who love their teams, living and dying on each win or loss.

In the midst of the seeming friendly banter in the fan bases, there is always tension and envy. Often hurt feelings and emotions get out of line. And, there are divided houses.

Every fan base is familiar with the vanity plates on the front of cars or flags in the front yard with the 'house divided' motif. When a Michigan fan marries a Michigan State fan, the house is sure to have unsettled times around the momentous weekends when the two teams meet in sport. In some cases, relationships become strained, while in others the rivalry spawns nothing more than sharp, humorous jabs. The house is said to be divided. Envy and jealousy of each other's successes is an undercurrent in even the most peaceful relations.

Scripture tells a similar story, though it has not been readily recognized until the last few decades. Writ large through the pages of scripture is an intriguing and glorious tale of envy, jealousy and competition that begins in Genesis and is not resolved until Revelation. Every biblical prophet touches on this story in some way, and many make the topic their only concern, yet for 2,000 years we have been largely oblivious to this wrestling match of a divided house.

There are a dozen or more overlapping motifs that reveal this intriguing story and the Father's unchanging plan and purpose. His purpose is to restore the Kingdom and have a nation of priests who reveal his glory to all of creation. Most students of scripture readily accept this as truth, but few understand *how* he is accomplishing his purposes, or even that this restoration is the single most prophesied event in scripture, *receiving even more direct mentions and allusions than the coming of the Messiah.*

In the following pages, I will seek to reveal the fullness of this topic and how scripture exposes it through direct statements, imagery, parable, and prophecy. I will share a story line that leads to the restoration of the most divided house in history. I will reveal the greater role of the Messiah beyond the traditional Christian understanding of his role as personal Savior. You will begin to understand the larger story of scripture, why so much of the Bible is both history and prophecy, how all of the pieces fit together, and how you fit in the greater picture of biblical history and the progress of redemption.

This journey on which we are embarking is one of intrigue, but more importantly, it is one of answers to many puzzling questions in the drama of human history. I invite you to step outside of traditional interpretation and discover a more complete picture of the whole flow of Hebrew history and the biblical record. At the center of that picture is the story of a divided house.

## A Father Divides His House

Before we can tackle this story at the center of history and understand how the house was divided, we must consider a picture presented in Genesis 32 and 33. For 20 years, Jacob had been out of the Land given to his grandfather Abraham. He had left with little more than his staff and the clothes on his back, but now he was returning with a large family, many offspring and thousands of sheep, goats, donkeys and camels. He had indeed been blessed and multiplied abundantly, but he was keenly aware of the dangers that lay ahead.

Scripture relates that, the night before crossing into the Land, he wrestled with "a man" whom Jacob himself attested to be an incarnation of the Lord (Genesis 32:24-28). This prophetic encounter foreshadows a future period known as the "time of Jacob's trouble" (Jeremiah 30:7), an era of extreme difficulty for the nation of Israel which Christians commonly call the Tribulation. What happened to Jacob during that encounter forever changed his life, and prefigures what will happen to the nation he fathered. When he refused to let his opponent go, the man touched his leg, dislocating the socket of his thigh and causing him to limp thereafter. Even that did not keep Jacob from clinging to his heavenly visitor, and from boldly requesting a blessing. The man agreed, changing Jacob's name to Israel, "prince of God," or "one who prevails with God." That name change brought with it assurance that Jacob and his seed would prevail, both in the trials immediately in front of him, and in the great trials to come throughout history, to the end of the ages.

When morning came, as Israel prepared to cross into the Land, he saw (in a vision perhaps?) his brother Esau and four hundred men coming for him. In a swift move to preserve his family, he divided them into two groups. His first wife, Leah, and her sons led the way over the river Jabbok, followed by his beloved second wife, Rachel, and her son, Joseph

Because we have not understood the larger overarching message of scripture, from beginning to end, we have assumed that this story was simply that: a story with a few spiritual lessons. And yet the magnitude of this prophetic picture cannot be overstated. The picture will become increasingly clear in the coming pages. For now, understand that we set this account before you to demonstrate that it is not unprecedented in scripture to see the father divide a family to convey them safely through danger and into the Promised Land. Not only does God the Father, by his will, take exactly the same action with all Israel, but he does so through the hands of Jacob!

Before we look at the actions performed by Jacob's hands, we must leap forward several centuries to the events of 1 Kings 12. Here we find the defining point in the history of Israel and the central part of a complex story that begins in Genesis and ends in Revelation. Without understanding 1 Kings 12 and its relation to the rest of scripture, we cannot rightly understand the Messiah, the Prophets, or the Apostles. Truly, we cannot rightly understand *any* of scripture. A bold statement, yes, but I will prove it true.

## A Kingdom Divided

Rehoboam inherited the world's most powerful and prosperous kingdom from his father, Solomon. Forty years of heavy taxation and state building projects had, however, taken their toll on Israel. Rebellion was in the air. Shortly after his coronation at Shechem, a large delegation of representatives from the northern ten tribes came to Rehoboam. Their request was simple:

> Your father made our yoke hard; now therefore lighten the hard service of your father and his heavy yoke which he put on us, and we will serve you." (1 Kings 12:4)

Rehoboam told them to "depart for three days, then . . . return to me on the third day." (I King 12:5, 12) During those three days, Rehoboam counseled with his old and wise advisers before foolishly settling on the advice of his young and inexperienced peers. Upon the return of the delegation from the northern tribes, Rehoboam foolishly promised to be harder on them than his father ever was.

The result of Rehoboam's decision was disastrous, but certainly not unexpected by men or by God. Scripture relates that when the northern tribes heard the decree, they immediately withdrew from Judah.

> When all Israel *saw* that the king did not listen to them, the people answered the king, saying,
>
> **"What portion do we have in David?** *We have* no inheritance in the son of Jesse; To your tents, O Israel! Now look after your own house, David!"
> So Israel departed to their tents. But as for the sons of Israel who lived in the cities of Judah, Rehoboam reigned over them. Then King Rehoboam sent Adoram, who was over the forced labor, and all Israel stoned him to death. And King Rehoboam made haste to mount his chariot to flee to Jerusalem. **So Israel has been in rebellion against the house of David to this day.** (1 Kings 12:16-19, emphasis added)

The prophet Ahijah had prophesied to Jeroboam the Ephraimite that ten parts of the Kingdom would be placed in his hands (1 Kings 11:31). Jeroboam was an industrious young man whom Solomon had previously charged with leading the forced labor from the House of Joseph – the tribes of Ephraim and Manasseh (1 Kings 11:26-40).[1] When the tribes rose in rebellion, the ambitious Jeroboam surfaced as the logical choice to rule over the newly-formed Northern Kingdom.

---

[1] I refer to a number of "houses" in this book, specifically the House of Jacob, House of Israel, House of Judah, House of Joseph, House of Ephraim, and House of David. This can be confusing for two reasons. First, there are so many that it can be difficult to keep them apart. Second, some of these terms refer interchangeably to the same group of people. I hope to make this clear as I go along. It is easy, though, to know who the House of Jacob is: they are the entire nation of Israel, the man whose name YHVH changed from Jacob to Israel as he was returning with his entire family ("house") to the Promised Land.

Although some are quick to declare that this rebellion and division was not of God, the scriptures say otherwise. Rehoboam gathered 180,000 chosen warriors of Judah and Benjamin to fight against the House of Israel and restore the kingdom, but before they could march out to war . . .

> . . . the word of God came to Shemaiah the man of God, saying, "Speak to Rehoboam the son of Solomon, king of Judah, and to all the house of Judah and Benjamin and to the rest of the people, saying, 'Thus says the LORD, "You must not go up and fight against your relatives the sons of Israel; return every man to his house, for **this thing has come from Me.**"'" So they listened to the word of the LORD, and returned and went *their way* according to the word of the LORD. (1 Kings 12:22-24, emphasis added)

Just as Ahijah had prophesied over Jeroboam that God would tear the kingdom apart and give ten pieces to Jeroboam, Shemaiah had confirmed that it was God's plan to divide the kingdom. As I will demonstrate, there are multiple specific reasons why the Father divided the kingdom, but first we need to understand that, according to Genesis 48 and 49, *the seeds of this separation were planted by Jacob himself.*

As we have seen, at the time of Jacob's troubles on the northern shore of the Jabbok, he wrestled with "a man" who changed his name from Jacob to Israel. Later, when Israel was old, his son Joseph, who had become Viceroy of Egypt, relocated his father and his entire family to Goshen. It is from his bed in Goshen that Israel sets the course of biblical and world history through several blessings and prophetic acts. The scriptures tell us:

> Now it came about after these things that Joseph was told, "Behold, your father is sick." So he took his two sons Manasseh and Ephraim with him. When it was told to Jacob, "Behold, your son Joseph has come to you," Israel collected his strength and sat up in the bed. (Genesis 48:1-2)

The details of the whole story in Genesis 48 are important, but I want us to focus on a couple of specific points in the latter half of the chapter. Israel blessed Joseph by blessing and adopting his two grandsons as his own sons, thus giving Joseph a double portion and the firstborn preeminence:

> But Israel stretched out his right hand and laid it on the head of Ephraim, who was the younger, and his left hand on Manasseh's head, **crossing his hands**, although Manasseh was the firstborn. He blessed Joseph, and said,
> "The God before whom my fathers Abraham and Isaac walked,
> The God who has been my shepherd all my life to this day,
> **The angel who has redeemed me** from all evil,
> Bless the lads;
> And may my name live on in them,
> And the names of my fathers Abraham and Isaac;
> And may they grow into a multitude in the midst of the earth." (Genesis 48:14-16, emphasis added)

As we will see, Ephraim and Manasseh have a special purpose and calling. Not only did Israel cross his hands in an odd move, placing the younger Ephraim ahead of Manasseh, but he also declared that the "angel who redeemed me" would be the one to bless the lads. This is a stunning prophecy involving the Angel of the Lord and the sign of the cross! Clarity would not come for 1500 or more years!

Joseph expressed displeasure at the elevation of Ephraim over Manasseh, but Israel is firm. He answers Joseph's concern by saying,

> "I know, my son, I know; he also will become a people and he also will be great. However, his younger brother shall be greater than he, and his descendants shall become **a multitude of nations.**" (Genesis 48:19, emphasis added)

As if the initial act wasn't shocking enough, Israel further clarifies by stating that Ephraim's descendants would be *melo hagoyim*, literally, the "fullness of the nations," or "fullness of the Gentiles"!

At that moment, the course and trajectory of the gospel of the kingdom was established, but before his death Israel would perform one final act that would set the drama of redemption in motion. He summoned all of his sons and explained to them what would befall them "in the latter days." (Genesis 49:1) In doing so, he broke with the tradition of giving both the headship and the firstborn blessing of abundance to the same son. Rather, Israel imparted headship – the scepter – to Judah, while heaping fruitfulness on Joseph by giving him the double portion of the firstborn (his two sons, Ephraim and Manasseh, would become fathers of tribes, along with their uncles), and the responsibility of carrying on the family name of Israel.

To Judah he says,

> "Judah, your brothers shall praise you;
> Your hand shall be on the neck of your enemies;
> Your father's sons shall bow down to you.
> Judah is a lion's whelp;
> From the prey, my son, you have gone up.
> He couches, he lies down as a lion,
> And as a lion, who dares rouse him up?
> The scepter shall not depart from Judah,
> Nor the ruler's staff from between his feet,
> Until Shiloh comes,
> And to him *shall be* the obedience of the peoples.
> He ties *his* foal to the vine,
> And his donkey's colt to the choice vine;
> He washes his garments in wine,
> And his robes in the blood of grapes.
> His eyes are dull from wine,
> And his teeth white from milk. (Genesis 49:8-12)

To Joseph he says,

> Joseph is a fruitful bough,
> A fruitful bough[2] by a spring;
> *Its* branches run over a wall.
> The archers bitterly attacked him,
> And shot *at him* and harassed him;

---

[2] The term translated "fruitful" is the Hebrew word *parah*, (פָּרָה, Strongs #H6509), which is the root of Ephraim, a name that means "doubly fruitful." The figurative meaning of the word "bough" is "son" or "sons." By using these words, Israel affirms yet again the fruitful blessing on Ephraim and his descendants, the sons of Joseph.

> But his bow remained firm,
> And his arms were agile,
> From the hands of the Mighty One of Jacob
> (From there is the Shepherd, the Stone of Israel),
> From the God of your father who helps you,
> And by the Almighty who blesses you
> *With* blessings of heaven above,
> Blessings of the deep that lies beneath,
> Blessings of the breasts and of the womb.
> The blessings of your father
> Have surpassed the blessings of my ancestors
> Up to the utmost bound of the everlasting hills;
> May they be on the head of Joseph,
> And on the crown of the head of the one distinguished
> among his brothers. (Genesis 49:22-26)

This blessing on Joseph is in addition to the blessing Jacob has bestowed on him previously. He had already given Joseph the double portion by making him the father of two tribes (Ephraim and Manasseh):

> "Now your two sons, who were born to you in the land of Egypt before I came to you in Egypt, are mine; Ephraim and Manasseh shall be mine, as Reuben and Simeon are." . . . Then Israel said to Joseph, "Behold, I am about to die, but God will be with you, and bring you back to the land of your fathers. **I give you one portion more than your brothers**, which I took from the hand of the Amorite with my sword and my bow." (Genesis 48:5, 21-22, emphasis added)

In the traditional practice, the firstborn received this double portion so that he had the resources to provide for the family as the new patriarch once the father had died. By his actions, however, Jacob declares that Joseph is to provide the resources that Judah is to administer wisely on behalf of the entire family.

As at the Jabbok, Jacob, now known as Israel, divides the family into two parts, the full manifestation of which does not occur until Jeroboam the Ephraimite is made king over the northern ten tribes. Scripture then begins to refer to this prophesied and divinely-directed division as the House of Israel, also known as the House of Ephraim, the House of Joseph, and simply Ephraim.[3]

But, why? Why divide the kingdom? It was clearly prophesied, and God himself declares that the division is of him. But, to what purpose?

A myopic view of history would regard this split as a disaster from the start. Jeroboam wasted no time in plunging the House of Israel into idolatry in clear violation of the Torah and the prophetic utterance of Ahijah. It is useful at this point to review that prophecy and find out exactly what Jeroboam was supposed to have done:

> It came about at that time, when Jeroboam went out of Jerusalem, that the prophet Ahijah the Shilonite found him on the road. Now Ahijah had clothed himself with a new cloak; and both of them were alone in the field. Then Ahijah took hold of the new cloak which was on him and tore it into twelve pieces. He said to Jeroboam, "Take for yourself ten pieces; for thus says the LORD, the God of Israel, 'Behold, I will tear the kingdom out of the hand of Solomon and give you ten tribes (but he will have one tribe, for the sake of My servant David and for the sake of Jerusalem, the city which I have chosen from all the tribes of Israel), because they have forsaken Me, and have worshiped Ashtoreth the goddess of the Sidonians, Chemosh the god of Moab, and Milcom the god of the sons of Ammon; and they have not walked in My ways, doing what is right in My sight and *observing* My statutes and My ordinances, as his father David *did*. Nevertheless I will not take the whole kingdom out of his hand, but I will make him ruler all the days of his life, for the sake of My servant David whom I chose, who observed My commandments and My statutes; but I will take the kingdom

---

[3] Since the terms House of Israel, House of Ephraim, and House of Joseph refer to the same group of people (e.g., Israelites of the Northern Kingdom; the Ten Tribes), from this point forward I will follow the precedent of scripture and use these terms interchangeably. In general, as I reference specific passages of scripture, I will use the name Israel, Ephraim, or Joseph that appears in each passage as we discuss it.

from his son's hand and give it to you, *even* ten tribes. But to his son I will give one tribe, that My servant David may have a lamp always before Me in Jerusalem, the city where I have chosen for Myself to put My name. **I will take you, and you shall reign over whatever you desire, and you shall be king over Israel. Then it will be, that if you listen to all that I command you and walk in My ways, and do what is right in My sight by observing My statutes and My commandments, as My servant David did, then I will be with you and build you an enduring house as I built for David, and I will give Israel to you.** Thus I will afflict the descendants of David for this, but not always.'" (1 Kings 11:29-39, emphasis added)

Sadly, Jeroboam did not abide by the terms of this prophetic declaration. As he consolidated his hold on the kingdom, Jeroboam sought ways to prevent his people from making pilgrimages to Jerusalem for the feasts or to make sacrifices. He instituted his own priesthood, his own places of worship, and his own feasts days. Essentially, he kept a form of worship of YHVH that was based on the Torah, but made significant changes that led the people away from Jerusalem and the House of David.[4]

Within a few short decades, the House of Israel had descended into gross idolatry and began receiving warnings from Prophets sent specifically to them. The southern House of Judah also committed abominations, but it was Israel, the House of Ephraim, that was prophesied to be scattered, while Judah would be preserved. Drawing a clear distinction between the houses and their respective fates, the prophet Hosea says:

> Then she [Hosea's wife] conceived again and gave birth to a daughter. And the LORD said to him, "Name her Lo-ruhamah [no mercy], for **I will no longer have compassion on the house of Israel**, that I would ever forgive them. But **I will**

---

[4] House of David is a term used consistently throughout Scripture to refer to the Davidic Dynasty. David is the king YHVH anointed to rule over the united Kingdom of Israel (1 Samuel 16:1-13). According to 2 Samuel 7:8-17 and 2 Kings 2:1-4, YHVH also promised that David's royal line would rule over Israel perpetually, meaning that Messiah would come from his descendants.

**have compassion on the house of Judah and deliver them** by the LORD their God, and will not deliver them by bow, sword, battle, horses or horsemen." (Hosea 1:6-7, emphasis added)

Jeremiah also foretold the distinct judgments God would inflict on Israel and Judah, saying:

> Then the LORD said to me in the days of Josiah the king, "Have you seen what faithless Israel did? She went up on every high hill and under every green tree, and she was a harlot there. I thought, 'After she has done all these things she will return to Me'; but she did not return, and her treacherous sister Judah saw it. And I saw that for all the adulteries of faithless Israel, **I had sent her away and given her a writ of divorce**, yet her treacherous sister Judah did not fear; but she went and was a harlot also. Because of the lightness of her harlotry, she polluted the land and committed adultery with stones and trees. Yet in spite of all this her treacherous sister Judah did not return to Me with all her heart, but rather in deception," declares the LORD. (Jeremiah 3:6-10, emphasis added)

Hosea confirms the divorce when he says,

> When she had weaned Lo-ruhamah, she conceived and gave birth to a son. And the LORD said, **"Name him Lo-ammi [not my people], for you are not My people and I am not your God."** (Hosea 1:8-9, emphasis added)

This is a devastating sentence levied against the House of Israel. No greater dishonor existed in the Ancient Near East than being "cut off" from the family. But Hosea continues with a word of hope:

> Yet the number of the sons of Israel will be like the sand of the sea, which cannot be measured or numbered; and in the place where it is said to them, "You are not My people," it will be said to them, "*You are* the sons of the living God." And the sons of Judah and the sons of Israel will be gathered together, and they will appoint for themselves one leader,

and they will go up from the land, for great will be the day of Jezreel. (Hosea 1:10-11)

In a wild twist that would puzzle the rabbis for centuries, Hosea proclaims that the House of Israel would not only be restored, but rejoined to the House of Judah! Their astonishment is justifiable; the Torah clearly says in Deuteronomy 24 that a divorced bride who has had relations with another man cannot return to her former husband.

> When a man takes a wife and marries her, and it happens that she finds no favor in his eyes because he has found some indecency in her, and he writes her a certificate of divorce and puts *it* in her hand and sends her out from his house, and she leaves his house and goes and becomes another man's *wife*, and if the latter husband turns against her and writes her a certificate of divorce and puts *it* in her hand and sends her out of his house, or if the latter husband dies who took her to be his wife, *then* her former husband who sent her away is not allowed to take her again to be his wife, since she has been defiled; for that is an abomination before the LORD, and you shall not bring sin on the land which the LORD your God gives you as an inheritance. (Deuteronomy 24:1-4)

Israel had clearly committed gross adultery on every high place. How, then, could she return to YHVH? Yet, the Lord through Jeremiah says,

> "Is Ephraim My dear son? Is he a delightful child? Indeed, as often as I have spoken against him, I certainly *still* remember him; therefore My heart yearns for him; I will surely have mercy on him," declares the LORD.
> "Set up for yourself roadmarks, place for yourself guideposts; direct your mind to the highway, the way by which you went. Return, O virgin of Israel, return to these your cities. (Jeremiah 31:20-21)

## JACOB'S TWELVE SONS

Jacob had twelve sons by his wives Leah and Rachel and his concubines Zilpah and Bilhah. The tribes of Israel are named for Jacob's sons and grandsons. Eleven of his sons became fathers of

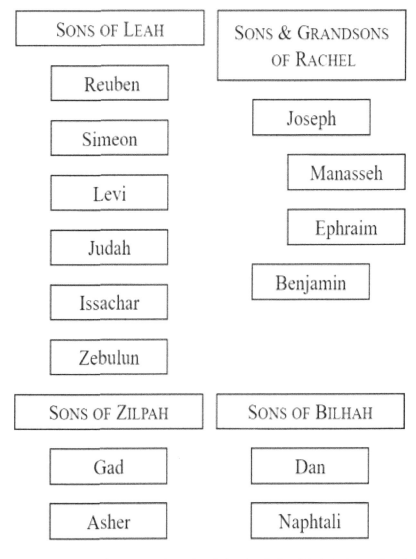

one tribe each, but Joseph, who inherited the birthright, gained a double portion when his two sons, Ephraim and Manasseh, became fathers of tribes as well (Genesis 48:8-22, 1 Chronicles 5:1-2).

# 2

# THE TEN TRIBES
# AND
# THE TWO TRIBES

**Seeing, and Not Seeing**

The fond memories I recall from my upbringing in a solid Christian family includes the stirring messages in song that imparted timeless truths of scripture into my heart and mind and soul as I sang them. They infused my being to a depth and breadth that sermons and Sunday School lessons could not approach. I may not have understood the full meaning of the songs, but the timeless truths contained within them have made them popular for centuries.

This is as true of Christmas carols as of Charles Wesley's immortal hymns. Although I no longer celebrate the Christmas holiday, I remain firmly attached to the Messiah whom I met at church. I first knew him as Jesus Christ; today I prefer to call him by his Hebrew name and title: Yeshua HaMashiach, or Messiah Yeshua.

I know Yeshua's Hebrew name thanks to a phenomenon sweeping the church in this generation. I call it the *Torah Awakening*, the growing awareness among Christians worldwide that the Law (God's Torah; his Law, Teaching, and Commandments as written by Moses in the first five books of the Bible) still applies today. This follows from the testimony of our Messiah himself:

> Do not think that I came to abolish the Law or the Prophets; I did not come to abolish but to fulfill. For truly I say to you, until heaven and earth pass away, not the smallest letter or stroke shall pass from the Law until all is accomplished. Whoever then annuls one of the least of these commandments, and teaches others *to do* the same, shall be

called least in the kingdom of heaven; but whoever keeps and teaches *them*, he shall be called great in the kingdom of heaven. (Matthew 5:17-19)

The Torah Awakening has created the need to rethink what we know of scripture, of the role (or roles) of Messiah, and of the definition of Israel. We have understood that Israel received the Torah, but as Christians, Israel was little more than a historical entity that provided the backdrop for our modern faith.

Except when we sang about it.

About 1,000 years ago, God inspired someone in Europe to write a song of praise in Latin which we know today as the Christmas carol, *O Come, O Come Emanuel*. The words spring straight from scripture, speaking to a national affiliation that Christians rarely acknowledge with the seriousness it requires:

*O come, O come, Emmanuel*
*And ransom captive Israel,*
*That mourns in lonely exile here*
*Until the Son God appear.*
*Rejoice! Rejoice! Emmanuel*
*Shall come to thee, O Israel.*

> *O come, O come, Thou Lord of might,*
> *Who to Thy tribes, on Sinai's height,*
> *In ancient times didst give the Law*
> *In cloud and majesty and awe.*
> *Rejoice! Rejoice! Emmanuel*
> *Shall come to thee, O Israel.*

*O come, Thou Rod of Jesse, free*
*Thine own from Satan's tyranny;*
*From depths of Hell Thy people save*
*And give them vict'ry o'er the grave.*
*Rejoice! Rejoice! Emmanuel*
*Shall come to thee, O Israel.*

> *O come, Thou Key of David, come,*
> *And open wide our heav'nly home*
> *Where all Thy saints with Thee shall dwell –*

> *O come, O come, Emmanuel.*
> *Rejoice! Rejoice! Emmanuel*
> *Shall come to thee, O Israel.*[1]

What does this song mean? Is it meant for Jews? After all, the prevailing opinion for the last 2,700 years has been that Jews are all there is to the nation of Israel. Why, then, do Jews not acknowledge Messiah Yeshua as their king?

The answer to that is complicated, and although the subject of this book touches it, a full investigation of the question is beyond its scope. Instead, let's investigate the application of *O Come, O Come Emanuel* to a different group of people: to Christians, a people who acknowledge the King of Israel, but who for the most part have not yet understood their identity as Israelites.

## Partaking of the Commonwealth?

This is one of those awkward situations we must think through if we are to understand the Torah Awakening. We tend to think of the Torah as only a Jewish thing. Is it? In practice, yes; only the Jews have attempted to remain faithful to the Law of God. Therefore they are rightly considered Israelites and Hebrews, not only because of physical descent from Israel's patriarchs Abraham, Isaac, and Jacob, but also because of their adherence to the Torah of Israel's God.[2]

---

[1] Kenneth W. Osbeck, *101 Hymn Stories* (Grand Rapids, Michigan: Kregel Publications, 1982), 177-178.

[2] It can be argued that Christians already keep much of the Torah. As Yeshua said, the weightier provisions of the Law are justice, mercy, and faithfulness (Matthew 23:23; see also Micah 6:8 and Deuteronomy 10:12-13). He also identified the two greatest commandments as loving God and loving others (Mark 12:28-31; see also Deuteronomy 6:4-5 and Leviticus 19:18). What most Christians do not do is keep the Sabbath on the seventh day (Saturday), celebrate the Feasts of the Lord (Passover, Pentecost, Tabernacles, etc.), eat a biblically clean diet per Leviticus 11, or wear *tzittzit* (tassles) on their garments to remind them of God's commandments (Numbers 15:37-41). These are the major provisions of Torah which Jews and Messianic/Hebraic followers of Yeshua honor, but which most Christians do not.

What, then, are we to make of Christians who keep Torah? For the most part, they call themselves something other than Christians, not because they have left Messiah Yeshua (the "Christ" in "Christian"), but because they have left the traditional church. Yet because they cling to Yeshua, the one who brought them into relationship with Almighty God, and who taught them to obey God's Torah, they cannot become Jews, nor do they desire to do so.

There is an answer staring us all right in the face. It appears not only in the Tanakh (Old Testament), but also throughout the Apostolic Writings (New Testament). The Apostle Paul explains this answer throughout his letters, but perhaps most clearly in his reference to the Commonwealth of Israel.

"Commonwealth" is from the Greek, *politeia* (πολίτης, Strongs #G4177), referring to a political entity like a state or nation. The term is used twice: once in Acts 22:28, when Paul refers to his own Roman citizenship; and a second time in Paul's letter to the Ephesians, when he refers to the citizenship of those who have attached themselves to Yeshua. The phrase in Ephesians is of particular interest to us. Here it is in context:

> Therefore remember that you, once Gentiles in the flesh—who are called Uncircumcision by what is called the Circumcision made in the flesh by hands—that at that time you were without Christ, being aliens from the **commonwealth of Israel** and strangers from the covenants of promise, having no hope and without God in the world. But now in Christ Jesus you who once were far off have been brought near by the blood of Christ. (Ephesians 2:11-13 NKJV, emphasis added)

This passage illustrates the reconciliation of non-Jews with Jews in an entity we could call "Greater Israel." The vehicle which makes that possible is the work of Messiah, who somehow makes the non-Jews acceptable to God and able to join with Jews in his Covenant.

Much of the reasoning presented here is based on passages from the Apostolic Writings. Jews, of course, do not acknowledge these documents as scripture, although there is an encouraging development among Jewish scholars to acknowledge the historical and cultural value of the New Testament. After all, most of the New Testament writers were Jewish, and all were knowledgeable of Torah and used it as their inspiration. One (Paul) was a disciple of Gamaliel, one of the most respected authorities on the Torah in first-century Judea (Acts 5:34, 22:3).[3] It seems, therefore, that any disagreement between Christians and Jews about the Apostolic Writings is not rooted in the godly principles stated throughout the Tanakh, but rather in their expectations of how Messiah is to fulfill those principles.[4]

Such is the case regarding the Commonwealth of Israel. The idea of the Commonwealth first appears in the Tanakh. It does include a commonly or jointly-held wealth, namely the Promised Land where the descendants of Abraham, Isaac, and Jacob are to live.

---

[3] Solomon Schecter and Wilhelm Bacher, "Gamaliel I," *Jewish Encyclopedia* (1906): accessed June 20, 2017, http://www.jewishencyclopedia.com/articles/6494-gamaliel-i; Francis Gigot, "Gamaliel," *The Catholic Encyclopedia*, vol 6 (1909): accessed June 30, 2017, http://www.newadvent.org/cathen/06374b.htm.

[4] Scholarly appreciation for the Apostolic Writings in some Jewish academic circles motivated the recent publication of *The Annotated Jewish New Testament*. In explaining their reasons for their undertaking, the editors state, "We believe that it is important for both Jews and non-Jews to understand how close, in many aspects, significant parts of the New Testament are to the Jewish practices and beliefs reflected in the works of the Dead Sea Scrolls, Philo and Josephus, the Pseudepigrapha and Deuterocanonical literature, the Targumim (Aramaic translations of the Bible), and slightly later rabbinic literature, and that the New Testament has, in many passages, Jewish origins. Jesus was a Jew, as was Paul; likely the authors known as Matthew and John were Jews, as were the authors of the Epistle of James and the book of Revelation. When they were writing, the 'parting of the ways' had not yet occurred. Other authors, such as the individual who composed the Gospel of Luke and the Acts of the Apostles, while probably not Jewish themselves, were profoundly influenced by first- and second-century Jewish thought and by the Jewish translations of the Tanakh into Greek, the Septuagint. Thus, understanding the diverse Jewish populations of the early Roman Empire–their habits, their conventions, their religious practices–is as crucial to understanding the New Testament writings as is general familiarity with the Roman world. In turn, familiarity with the New Testament helps Jews to recover some of our own history." Amy-Jill Levine and Marc Zvi Brettler, eds., *The Jewish Annotated New Testament* (New York: Oxford University Press, 2011), xi.

However, it includes far more than that: a restored relationship with the Living God through the Covenant he established with Abraham.

The Bible explains how all of humanity rejected this relationship with the Creator, first in the Garden of Eden, then in the wicked global civilization that God judged to destruction in the Great Flood, and afterward in the disastrous demonstration of human pride at the Tower of Babel (Genesis 3:1-24, 6:1-8, 11:1-9). Rather than destroy humanity completely, God implemented a plan of redemption through Abraham, a man whom God called for that specific purpose (Genesis 12:1-3). That Abraham obeyed God's Torah is evident from what the Creator himself said when he renewed the Covenant with Abraham's son Isaac:

> I will multiply your descendants as the stars of heaven, and will give your descendants all these lands; and by your descendants all the nations of the earth shall be blessed; **because Abraham obeyed Me and kept My charge, My commandments, My statutes and My laws.** (Genesis 26:4-5, emphasis added)

Abraham became the first to hear and obey God's Torah long before it was given formally at Mount Sinai to the nation of Israel that he fathered. By taking God at his word and following through with actions, Abraham demonstrated the basis of covenant relationship for all generations. That is why Moses and the Apostles could point to Abraham as the model for faith leading to salvation: "Abraham believed God, and it was credited to him as righteousness" (Genesis 15:6, Romans 4:3, 20-22, Galatians 3:6, James 2:23).

As God promised, Abraham did become the father of a multitude of nations (Genesis 17:4). However, the redeeming seed of the Covenant passed directly through his son Isaac and grandson Jacob to the nation of Israel (Genesis 17:18-19, 25:19-26, 27:1-40, 32:24-28). Even though the nation disobeyed God, incurring his severe judgment, his faithfulness to the Covenant with Abraham and Abraham's seed ensured he would preserve them forever. This is evident in passages such as these:

> Then the LORD will have compassion on Jacob and again choose Israel, and settle them in their own land, then strangers will join them and attach themselves to the house of Jacob. (Isaiah 14:1)
>
> I permitted Myself to be sought by those who did not ask *for Me*; I permitted Myself to be found by those who did not seek Me. I said, "Here am I, here am I," to a nation which did not call on My name. (Isaiah 65:1)

These passages indicate that Christian tradition is in error in the supposition that God created two entities by which he deals with humanity, namely Israel and the church. "Church" is a rendition of the Greek word *ekklesia* (ἐκκλησία; Strongs #G1577), the congregation or assembly of God. *Ekklesia* corresponds to the Hebrew *qahal* (קָהָל; Strongs #H6950), a term used throughout the Tanakh to refer to the congregation or assembly of all Israel.

The evidence of scripture indicates that God created only one covenant entity: the family, congregation, body, nation, and kingdom called Israel. His purpose since the days of Abraham has been to establish a way for all nations to be brought into fellowship with himself through the nation of Israel. From the beginning, Israel was destined to become a "kingdom of priests" (Exodus 19:6) that would serve as a vehicle of salvation for all the nations.

What we have not recognized, until now, is that to complete His work, the family had to be divided.

Various church doctrines over the ages have emphasized the global salvation mission of Israel, but have failed to explain adequately how the church could fulfill that role, or how the Jewish people fit into this picture. This has led to the error of Replacement Theology, which asserts that the church is now "Spiritual Israel," and that Jews are no longer relevant in God's plan except in terms of the wrath yet to be poured out on them and the rest of the unbelieving world during the Great Tribulation.

Paul's use of the term, Commonwealth of Israel, is *not* Replacement Theology. It is an understanding that Jews and Christians each play a part in God's plan, and that the two must join together to display the fullness of his Counsels. Christians do not *replace* the Jewish people, but instead *join with* Jews in the fulfillment of God's plan for all humanity. This is based on the writings of Paul that those who believe in Yeshua as Messiah are the seed of Abraham. He presents this train of logic in Romans 9:6-8 and Galatians 3:15-29, culminating in this assertion:

> And if you belong to Christ, then you are Abraham's descendants [seed], heirs according to promise. (Galatians 3:29)

Paul *does not* state here that non-Jewish believers in Yeshua have replaced Jews as the seed of Abraham. Instead, he affirms that non-Jews now have a place *alongside* Jews in the promises of God. In Romans 11, he draws the symbol of an olive tree from Jeremiah 11:15-16 as a representation of Israel to illustrate this point. He plainly states that those from the nations (Gentiles) have been grafted into the tree by virtue of their belief in Israel's Messiah, and therefore have full part with Jews, the "natural branches" of the tree. In other words, to paraphrase Paul's statement in Romans 9:6, **all Jews are Israelites, but not all Israelites are Jews**.

God is not finished with Israel. In fact, Israel is much bigger than both Jews and Christians commonly suppose.

## Introducing the Two Witnesses

But let us back up for a moment. Why is it so important to be part of Israel? We begin to understand this from the testimony of Moses and the Prophets:

> See, I have taught you statutes and judgments just as the LORD my God commanded me, that you should do thus in the land where you are entering to possess it. So keep and do *them*, for that is your wisdom and your understanding in the sight of the peoples who will hear all these statutes and say, "Surely this great nation is a wise and understanding people." **For what great nation is there that has a god so near to it as is the LORD our God whenever we call on Him? Or what great nation is there that has statutes and**

**judgments as righteous as this whole law which I am setting before you today?** (Deuteronomy 4:5-8, emphasis added)

He declares His words to Jacob,
His statutes and His ordinances to Israel.
**He has not dealt thus with any nation;**
**And as for His ordinances, they have not known them.**
Praise the LORD! (Psalm 147:19-20, emphasis added)

"Fear not, O Jacob My servant," declares the LORD, "and do not be dismayed, O Israel; for behold, I will save you from afar and your offspring from the land of their captivity. And Jacob will return and will be quiet and at ease, and no one will make him afraid. **For I am with you," declares the LORD, "to save you; for I will destroy completely all the nations where I have scattered you, only I will not destroy you completely.** But I will chasten you justly and will by no means leave you unpunished.' (Jeremiah 30:10-11, emphasis added)

If we have a question about Israeli exceptionalism, we have to take that up with YHVH himself. It is his idea. Not only is Israel the one nation of all the nations on earth that God has chosen as his own special possession, but according to Jeremiah's prophecy it is the only one that will survive when the Almighty pours out his just wrath on a rebellious world. Discerning people would be wise to find some way to become part of the nation of Israel before that happens.

But how? Isn't Israel Jewish? And to become an Israelite, or Israeli, doesn't a person have to convert to Judaism?

Let us repeat this fundamental truth: *all Jews are Israelites, but not all Israelites are Jews*. There is a large part of the nation of Israel that is not now, never has been, and never will be Jewish.

At its foundation, the nation of Israel consisted of twelve tribes. Only one of those Twelve Tribes, namely, the tribe of Judah (Yehudah, יְהוּדָה, Strongs #H3063) could be considered Jewish. In fact, Judah is the origin of the name Jew.

When God divided the Israel into two political entities, ten of those non-Jewish tribes followed Jeroboam, leader of the tribe of Ephraim, in establishing the Northern Kingdom which became known as Israel (1 Kings 11-12; 2 Chronicles 10). Only one tribe – Benjamin – remained loyal to Rehoboam, grandson of King David, and stayed in political union with Judah. Judah and Benjamin, plus most of the priestly tribe of Levi, along with a remnant of loyal Hebrews from the other tribes, comprised the Southern Kingdom, which took the name of Judah. Today, the Jewish people are for the most part descendants of this Southern Kingdom.

Interestingly, the first mention of Jews in scripture is in 2 Kings, in the context of war between Israel and Judah:

> Then Rezin king of Syria and Pekah son of Remaliah king of Israel came up to Jerusalem to war: and they besieged Ahaz [king of Judah], but could not overcome him. At that time Rezin king of Syria recovered Elath to Syria, and drave the Jews from Elath: and the Syrians came to Elath, and dwelt there unto this day. (2 Kings 16:5-6, KJV)

Many translations do not use "Jews" in this passage, opting instead for "men of Judah" (ESV, NKJV), "people of Judah" (NIV), or "Judeans" (CJB, NASB, NRSV). Regardless which terms are used, this passage makes a distinction between the Yehudim (Jews) and the other Israelites who allied with the Syrians (or *Arameans* in some translations) and attacked them. In fact, the war reported in 2 Kings 16 and in the more detailed account in 2 Chronicles 28:1-15, forms the backdrop for a series of Messianic prophecies given through Isaiah. These prophecies commence in Isaiah 7, immediately after the prophet records his dramatic vision of the Lord in the Temple, and commission to carry YHVH's message to all the people of Israel. They include this familiar promise:

> Therefore the Lord Himself will give you a sign: Behold, a virgin will be with child and bear a son, and she will call His name Immanuel." (Isaiah 7:14)

Matthew 1:23 refers to this prophecy of Messiah's birth. That much we understood from our upbringing in church. What we never learned was that Isaiah gave this prophecy in the context of a war between the two divided kingdoms of Israel. Throughout the prophecy, Isaiah also makes a point of referring to these two Israelite entities by the names of their chief tribes: Ephraim and Judah.

These are the two Houses of Israel, the two divisions of God's Kingdom which comprise the Two Witnesses of the Almighty and his Covenant.

**Cut Out of the Kingdom**

As I will explain, the message of YHVH's Kingdom is incomplete without the testimony of *both witnesses*. Where this testimony became garbled over the centuries is partly due to the fact that Isaiah's prophecy came true: within a generation, the Northern Kingdom of Israel ceased to exist. Thereafter, reference to the Jews in scripture became frequent as they alone remained to carry on the testimony of Israel.

Yet they are not alone. The other House is still out there, and will return as the Lord himself clearly promises. In fact, Isaiah makes this promise soon after his prophecy of Ephraim's destruction:

> Then it will happen on that day that the Lord will again recover the second time with His hand the remnant of His people, who will remain, from Assyria, Egypt, Pathros, Cush, Elam, Shinar, Hamath, and from the islands of the sea. And He will lift up a standard for the nations and assemble the banished ones of Israel, and will gather the dispersed of Judah from the four corners of the earth. **Then the jealousy of Ephraim will depart, and those who harass Judah will be cut off; Ephraim will not be jealous of Judah, and Judah will not harass Ephraim.** (Isaiah 11:10-13-16, emphasis added)

This Messianic prophecy begins with reference to the Root of Jesse, the one on whom the Seven Spirits of God rest (Isaiah 11:1-2; Revelation 3:1). How interesting that it is given in the context of the Lord restoring his chosen people: Ephraim and Judah.

The prophecy is specific: there are two parts of Israel which must be restored. Both have been scattered to the four corners of the earth, but whereas one (Judah) has been dispersed, the other (Ephraim) has been banished. The difference is this: although the Jewish people have been driven from the Promised Land into every part of the world, they have retained their Israelite identity. In contrast, Ephraim (non-Jewish Israel) was not only exiled from the Land, but cut out of the Kingdom altogether (Jeremiah 3:6-8; Hosea 1:6-7). Yet God promises to bring them back as a distinct entity, rejoin them with Judah, and restore his Covenant Nation in the Messianic Kingdom of the Son of David.

It will be a miracle beyond belief. Not only because the national entity called Ephraim has not existed for over 2,700 years, but also because there is tremendous opposition to Ephraim's return. Oddly enough, the opposition comes not primarily from without, but *from within the ranks of God's own people.*

This is the point of Isaiah's cryptic words about the animosity between the two Houses:

> Then the jealousy of Ephraim will depart, and those who harass Judah will be cut off; Ephraim will not be jealous of Judah, and Judah will not harass Ephraim. (Isaiah 11:13)

The jealousy of Ephraim is in the fact that Judah is the designated leader of the nation even though Ephraim carries the birthright and the name of the family (Israel). That division of honor and responsibility originated with Jacob, patriarch of the nation, when he blessed his sons and grandsons just before he died (Genesis 48-49). Ephraim and the tribes with them resented the fact that their wealth and power would always fall under the dominion of Judah's headship. In time, that resentment exploded into rebellion against the dynasty of David, the king YHVH chose from the tribe of Judah to rule over the entire nation. To this day, the resentment manifests in the form of attempts by various segments of the church to usurp Judah's place in the nation and claim to be the new, or spiritual, Israel. If, as I believe, Ephraim today exists largely within Christianity, then this tendency has deep and ancient roots.

But what is the vexation of Judah toward Ephraim? Simply put, it is the tendency to exclude Ephraim from participation in the nation of Israel. Perhaps the clearest statement on this subject comes from Ezekiel, a prophet who spoke both to the House of Israel (then in exile over 120 years) and to the House of Judah (in the process of being exiled to Babylon):

> Then the word of the LORD came to me, saying, "Son of man, your brothers, your relatives, your fellow exiles and the whole house of Israel, all of them, *are those* to whom the inhabitants of Jerusalem have said, **'Go far from the LORD; this land has been given us as a possession.'"** (Ezekiel 11:14-15, emphasis added)

At the time Ezekiel received this prophecy, Jerusalem was still the capital of Judah. The inhabitants of Jerusalem were Jews of the House of Judah. Their words, as the prophet states, were directed against their exiled kin of the House of Israel, charging that they no longer had a place within the nation.

That is the vexation of Judah toward Ephraim. From that day to this, the only way a person can be admitted to the nation of Israel is on Jewish terms, which means conversion to Judaism. In the first century, the applicable term was "circumcision," which involved every part of the Rabbinic conversion process (including physical circumcision).

It has mattered little that Ephraimites would retain a memory of YHVH in their wanderings. That, too, is part of Ezekiel's prophecy:

> "Therefore say, 'Thus says the Lord GOD, "**Though I had removed them far away among the nations and though I had scattered them among the countries, yet I was a sanctuary for them a little while in the countries where they had gone.**"' Therefore say, 'Thus says the Lord GOD, "I will gather you from the peoples and assemble you out of the countries among which you have been scattered, and I will give you the land of Israel."' When they come there, they will remove all its detestable things and all its abominations from it. **And I will give them one heart, and**

**put a new spirit within them. And I will take the heart of stone out of their flesh and give them a heart of flesh, that they may walk in My statutes and keep My ordinances and do them. Then they will be My people, and I shall be their God.** But as for those whose hearts go after their detestable things and abominations, I will bring their conduct down on their heads," declares the Lord GOD. (Ezekiel 11:16-21, emphasis added)

Astute readers will recognize here the components of the New Covenant: the radical heart change God himself brings about in his people. It is a transformation addressed throughout the scriptures, from Moses to Jeremiah to Paul (Deuteronomy 30:6; Jeremiah 31:31-34; Romans 12:1-2).

This is the testimony of Israel/Ephraim: to wander the earth with a cultural memory of the Holy God who redeemed them from slavery in Egypt, and who will redeem them again from the exile imposed for their rebellion. As they mixed with the peoples of the earth, Ephraimites leavened the nations with the leaven of the Kingdom of Heaven, ready to respond when the good news of salvation and redemption through Yeshua came to them. Although they did not know their Israelite identity, they accepted the testimony that Yeshua is God's provision to bring them into covenantal relationship with him. Moreover, they knew that anyone could avail themselves of that offer of redemption.

This good news is something that Judah has for the most part not recognized. Sadly, it is something Judah has hindered for nearly 2,000 years. Not the salvation part; that, according to prevailing Jewish opinion, is fine for Christians and for Gentiles in general, but not for Jews, who have their own relationship with the Almighty. What is a problem is when these non-Jews claim to be part of the nation of Israel. Such claims, it appears, threaten Jewish identity as Israelites, perhaps even generating fear that a flood of Gentiles coming into the nation will overwhelm the Jews and make them an irrelevant minority.

The fear is not unfounded, as 2,000 years of Christian-Jewish relations have demonstrated. It seems both sides have had incentive to remain apart. If this Gospel of the Kingdom really does mean a reunification of the two Houses of Israel into a (re)newed national entity of Twelve Tribes under the Son of David, then it means the religious orders of both sides must undergo radical restructuring. Given the tremendous wealth and political power that have accumulated in the Christian and Jewish worlds through their existence as related, and yet distinct, religions, it is no surprise that the existing order is something both sides prefer to maintain.

Hence the dilemma of Christian support to Israel. If we carry this to the logical conclusion, and the two are to become one, then either Christians must become Jews, or Jews must become Christians.

Unless there is another alternative: an alternative which adjusts our understanding of Israel to encompass far more than we have heretofore understood.

This is an Israel of two reunited Houses, living as Hebrews under the Torah of the Living God, as administered by their King-Messiah Son of David.

It is an Israel that contains much of what Judaism and Christianity hold as true, because it is true.

It is an Israel that completes the vision of both Judaism and Christianity, unraveling those knotty dilemmas each have been unable to decipher completely or satisfactorily within their own paradigms.

This is the Israel in which the Ten Tribes and the Two Tribes cease their warfare and submit to their King.

## ISRAEL'S TWO HOUSES

The two chief tribes in the nation of Israel are Judah and Joseph. As 1 Chronicles 5:1-2 explains, Judah received the blessing from Jacob to be the ruler of the entire family, while Joseph received the

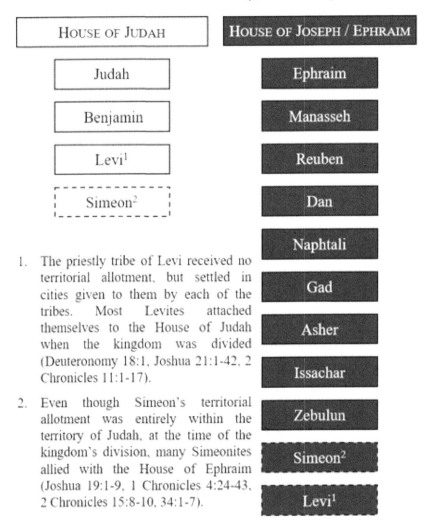

| HOUSE OF JUDAH | HOUSE OF JOSEPH / EPHRAIM |
|---|---|
| Judah | Ephraim |
| Benjamin | Manasseh |
| Levi[1] | Reuben |
| Simeon[2] | Dan |
|  | Naphtali |
|  | Gad |
|  | Asher |
|  | Issachar |
|  | Zebulun |
|  | Simeon[2] |
|  | Levi[1] |

1. The priestly tribe of Levi received no territorial allotment, but settled in cities given to them by each of the tribes. Most Levites attached themselves to the House of Judah when the kingdom was divided (Deuteronomy 18:1, Joshua 21:1-42, 2 Chronicles 11:1-17).

2. Even though Simeon's territorial allotment was entirely within the territory of Judah, at the time of the kingdom's division, many Simeonites allied with the House of Ephraim (Joshua 19:1-9, 1 Chronicles 4:24-43, 2 Chronicles 15:8-10, 34:1-7).

firstborn blessing and the family name (Israel). The House of Joseph is often called Ephraim, after Joseph's son who became father of the chief tribe of the House of Joseph.

# 3

# HOUSE OF ISRAEL
# ≠
# HOUSE OF JUDAH

**All Jews Are Israelites, But Not All Israelites Are Jews**

Christianity and Judaism share a common misperception. The assumption is that whenever "House of Israel" and/or "House of Judah" appear in scripture, the terms refer to the same group of people. Growing up in a Christian home, I was reared in that paradigm, with the result that many passages of scripture were perplexing and nearly indecipherable. But then God began to open my eyes to the fact that he had a purpose in drawing a distinction between these separate groups of people, revealing that he had a different role and task for each house.

Before I go further, I should make something clear. When I refer to the House of Judah, I mean both the ancient Kingdom of Judah that remained loyal to the Davidic Dynasty, and the Jewish people who are descended from them. Judah and the Jewish people are one and the same. All of them are Israelites, and that is where I agree with the commonly held view of Judaism and Christianity (and the rest of the world for that matter).

My disagreement is with the commonly held view that the Jewish people are both the House of Judah *and* the House of Israel. When I refer to the House of Israel, House of Joseph, and House of Ephraim, I am referring to the non-Jewish part of God's family, *who are* also *Israelites,* either by birth or by being grafted in.

This is the paradigm-shifting thought. The world until now has assumed that the Jews are Israel and Israel is the Jews; that the division of the human race is between Jews and Gentiles. What the scriptures explain, however, is that the real division is between *Israelites/Hebrews* and Gentiles.

By way of illustration, consider the example of the United States of America. To the rest of the world, all of us were born here or who have been naturalized as citizens are Americans. That is correct. However, within this group of 330 million people who may be called Americans, only 28 million reside in the state of Texas. Although all Texans are Americans, it is not correct to say that all Americans are Texans.

The reason the world does not yet recognize non-Jewish Hebrews is because they have not existed as a people for about 2,700 years. For nearly three millennia, the Jewish people – the House of Judah – have been the only visible portion of the nation of Israel. It is understandable that the scriptures referring to the two Houses are a mystery to Christians, because Christianity has no expectation that the "Lost Tribes" of the House of Israel/Joseph/Ephraim will ever return. Jews do expect the Lost Tribes to return, but they expect them to be (or become) Jewish. Very few seem to expect that the Two Houses of Israel will manifest as two distinct entities prior to Messiah's coming to reunite them.

**Two Houses, One Kingdom**

The record of scripture is clear. Let us now turn to some of the passages that demonstrate the House of Israel and the House of Judah are not and cannot be the same.

I have already cited the example of Hosea 1:6-7:

> Then she conceived again and gave birth to a daughter. And the LORD said to him, "Name her Lo-ruhamah [No Mercy], for **I will no longer have compassion on the house of Israel**, that I would ever forgive them. But **I will have compassion on the house of Judah and deliver them** by the LORD their God, and will not deliver them by bow, sword, battle, horses or horsemen." (Hosea 1:6-7, emphasis added)

Clearly, the House of Israel and the House of Judah cannot be the same group of people. One receives compassion, the other does not. Hosea has multiple similarly distinctive verses, such as this one:

> Though you, **Israel**, play the harlot, do not let **Judah** become guilty; also do not go to Gilgal, or go up to Bethaven and take the oath: "As the LORD lives!" (Hosea 4:15, emphasis added)

And this verse from Hosea 5:

> Moreover the pride of **Israel** testifies against him, and **Israel and Ephraim** stumble in their iniquity; **Judah also** has stumbled with them. (Hosea 5:5, emphasis added)

We have already seen the distinction drawn between the House of Israel and the House of Judah in 1 Kings 12:20-24, but it existed well before Rehoboam's time. The division is visible in 2 Samuel 2 during the years following the death of King Saul.

> But Abner the son of Ner, commander of Saul's army, had taken Ish-bosheth the son of Saul and brought him over to Mahanaim. He made him king over Gilead, over the Ashurites, over Jezreel, over Ephraim, and over Benjamin, even over **all Israel**. Ish-bosheth, Saul's son, was forty years old when he became king over Israel, and he was king for two years. **The house of Judah, however, followed David.** The time that David was king in Hebron over the house of Judah was seven years and six months. (2 Samuel 2:8-11, emphasis added)

Judah, quite logically, followed David because he was of the tribe of Judah. Some of them may have understood Jacob's prophecy that the scepter would not depart from Judah. Similarly, some in the rest of Israel may have understood the prophecy of fruitfulness and the firstborn blessing on Joseph/Ephraim. The tribe of Issachar seems to have had a particular aptitude for such things. As the tide turned in David's favor, and the tribes began to acknowledge his claim to the throne, Issachar was among the first to do so:

> Of the sons of Issachar, men who understood the times, with knowledge of what Israel should do, their chiefs *were* two hundred; and all their kinsmen *were* at their command. (2 Chronicles 12:32)

We may infer that understanding of the times meant realization that Judah, through David, was at last ready to take up the scepter, and that Joseph/Ephraim would entrust him to administer the wealth and resources they contributed to the united kingdom.

Nevertheless, the competition between the two Houses has never abated. The prophet Isaiah records a yet-unfulfilled prophecy that is beginning to take shape in our day. He says,

> Then it will happen **on that day** that the Lord will again recover **the second time** with His hand the remnant of His people, who will remain, from Assyria, Egypt, Pathros, Cush, Elam, Shinar, Hamath, and from the islands of the sea. And He will lift up a standard for the nations and **assemble the banished ones of Israel**, and will **gather the dispersed of Judah** from the four corners of the earth. Then **the jealousy of Ephraim** will depart, and **those who harass Judah** will be cut off; **Ephraim will not be jealous of Judah, and Judah will not harass Ephraim**. They will swoop down on the slopes of the Philistines on the west; together they will plunder the sons of the east; they will possess Edom and Moab, and the sons of Ammon will be subject to them. (Isaiah 11:11-14, emphasis added)

This passage is in the early stages of fulfillment even now. Judah is being gathered to the Land. Some might claim that the mention of Ephraim is parallelism – that Ephraim is only another way to refer to the Jewish people. That, however, is a wholly unsatisfactory solution, not only because Judah and Ephraim are distinct parts of Israel, but because there has been no visible fulfillment of Ephraim's return. If we were to poll 10,000 Israelis as to whether they are of Judah or Ephraim, how many would claim anything other than Judah? We suggest that the numbers would be very few indeed.

Yet in the Two Stick prophecy of Ezekiel 37, God declares that this is the unification of two peoples, two kingdoms! He promises:

> I will make them one nation in the land, on the mountains of Israel; and one king will be king for all of them; and **they will no longer be two nations and no longer be divided into two kingdoms.** (Ezekiel 37:22, emphasis added)

If we look in the world today, we see the House of Judah established as the modern State of Israel, but who is the other? Where are they?

Jeremiah further draws distinction between the two Houses in multiple places. Chapter 3 is incredibly direct, as we have seen:

> Then the LORD said to me in the days of Josiah the king, "Have you seen what **faithless Israel** did? She went up on every high hill and under every green tree, and she was a harlot there. I thought, 'After she has done all these things she will return to Me'; but she did not return, and **her treacherous sister Judah** saw it. And I saw that for all the adulteries of **faithless Israel**, I had sent her away and given her a writ of divorce, yet **her treacherous sister Judah** did not fear; but she went and was a harlot also. Because of the lightness of her harlotry, she polluted the land and committed adultery with stones and trees. Yet in spite of all this **her treacherous sister Judah** did not return to Me with all her heart, but rather in deception," declares the LORD. (Jeremiah 3:6-10, emphasis added)

Ezekiel echoes this distinction in chapter 23 as he tells of two sisters, Oholah and Oholibah, specifically connecting them with the capital cities of the two kingdoms:

> Their names were Oholah the elder and Oholibah her sister. And they became Mine, and they bore sons and daughters. And *as for* their names, Samaria is Oholah and Jerusalem is Oholibah. (Ezekiel 23:4)

In Ezekiel 4, the prophet articulates differing judgments for their varying degrees of sin:

Now you son of man, get yourself a brick, place it before you and inscribe a city on it, Jerusalem. Then lay siege against it, build a siege wall, raise up a ramp, pitch camps and place battering rams against it all around. Then get yourself an iron plate and set it up as an iron wall between you and the city, and set your face toward it so that it is under siege, and besiege it. This is a sign to the house of Israel. **As for you, lie down on your left side and lay the iniquity of the house of Israel on it**; you shall bear their iniquity for the number of days that you lie on it. For I have assigned you a number of days corresponding to the years of their iniquity, **three hundred and ninety days; thus you shall bear the iniquity of the house of Israel**. When you have completed these, **you shall lie down a second time, *but* on your right side and bear the iniquity of the house of Judah; I have assigned it to you for forty days, a day for each year**. (Ezekiel 4:1-6, emphasis added)

As we return to Jeremiah 3, we see two more verses demonstrating the impossibility that the two are the same or some form of parallel mention. Jeremiah says:

And the LORD said to me, "**Faithless Israel** has proved herself more righteous than **treacherous Judah**. (Jeremiah 3:11, emphasis added)

In those days the **house of Judah** will walk with the **house of Israel**, and **they will come together** from the land of the north to the land that I gave your fathers as an inheritance. (Jeremiah 3:18, emphasis added)

These verses, like so many others, simply cannot be speaking of the same body of people. Because of the persistence of the "House of Israel = House of Judah" mindset, both in Judaism and in Christianity, this point cannot be overstated: scripture states repeatedly that they are two groups of people with differing destinies who are brought back together at the end of days!

Besides passages that draw distinction between the houses, there are verses that can only reasonably be applied to one house or the other, but not both. Several examples are:

> Moreover, the LORD will scatter you among all peoples, from one end of the earth to the other end of the earth; and there **you shall serve other gods, wood and stone**, which you or your fathers have not known. (Deuteronomy 28:64, emphasis added.)

> I, even I, am He who comforts you. Who are you that you are afraid of man who dies and of the son of man who is made like grass, that **you have forgotten the LORD your Maker**, Who stretched out the heavens and laid the foundations of the earth, that you fear continually all day long because of the fury of the oppressor, as he makes ready to destroy? But where is the fury of the oppressor? (Isaiah 51:12-13, emphasis added)

> "Surely, as a woman treacherously departs from her lover, so you have dealt treacherously with Me, **O house of Israel**," declares the LORD.
> A voice is heard on the bare heights, the weeping *and* the supplications of the sons of Israel; because they have perverted their way, **they have forgotten the LORD their God**. Return, O **faithless sons**, I will heal your faithlessness."
> "Behold, we come to You; for You are the LORD our God." (Jeremiah 3:20-22, emphasis added)

Have the Jewish people served other gods, wood and stone? For the most part, no – at least not since the end of the Babylonian Captivity. Who can argue that the Jewish people since that time have forgotten their Covenant with God, or that they worshipped idols of wood and stone? Certainly, they have not acted perfectly, but the hallmark of their reputation is that in the face of terrible persecution, they have clung, at times desperately, to the Covenant and Torah, with the expectation of God being true to his everlasting Word.

The House of Israel/Joseph/Ephraim, however, has had a chronic issue of service to other gods, or to YHVH as represented by images of wood and stone – a practice he does not appreciate. It is the House of Israel who was assimilated into hundreds of peoples and cultures, and who subsequently forgot their God and abandoned the Torah.

Verses such as these demonstrate particular fulfillment of prophecy for one House or the other. As we recognize God's purpose in dividing the Houses and guiding them into their respective destinies, passages like these become increasingly clear and literal in their fulfillment.

Without belaboring the point, it is sufficient to say that scripture contains enough passages articulating a distinction between the two Houses that we cannot assume each reference is just another poetic name for the Jewish people. *Every* use of the related names for the two Houses must be carefully weighed by the surrounding context to determine which part of the nation is the subject in each case. When one does so, yet more specific differences between the two Houses begin to manifest. Scripture comes into sharper focus as we begin to understand God's plan and purpose for his two witnesses in the earth.

## TRIBAL ALLOTMENTS AFTER THE CONQUEST OF CANAAN

Jesse Lyman Hurlbut, *Bible atlas: a manual of Biblical geography and history, especially prepared for the use of teachers and students of the Bible and for Sunday school instruction, containing maps, plans, review charts, colored diagrs. and illustrated with accurate views of the principal cities and localities known to Bible history* (Chicago: Rand, McNally, 1910), 55.

# 4

# A TALE OF TWOS

*On the evidence of two or three witnesses a matter shall be confirmed. (Deuteronomy 19:15)*

*By the mouth of two or three witnesses every fact may be confirmed. (Matthew 18:16)*

*Every fact is to be confirmed by the testimony of two or three witnesses. (2 Corinthians 13:1)*

Twos. The scriptures are full of twos that point over and over in a unified direction to a singular pair of twos.

Consider this list of twos:

| | | |
|---|---|---|
| Two Witnesses | Moses & Elijah | Mal 4:4-6, Matt 17:1-8 |
| | Two Olive Trees | Zech 4:1-7, Rev 11:3-6 |
| | Two Candlesticks | Zech 4:1-7, Rev 11:3-6 |
| | Heaven & Earth | Deut 4:26, Matt 5:18 |
| | Law & Prophets | 2 Kings 17:13, Matt 5:17, Romans 3:21 |
| | Spirit and Truth | Psalm 31:5, John 4:23-24 |
| Two Leavened Loaves at Shavuot | | Leviticus 23:15-17, 1 Samuel 10:1-4 |
| Two Silver Trumpets | | Numbers 10:2-3 |
| Two Sisters | Oholah & Oholibah | Ezekiel 23 |
| Two Sons | Prodigal & Elder Brother | Luke 15:11-32 |
| Two Sticks | Judah & Ephraim | Ezekiel 37:15-28 |
| Two Families | Judah & Ephraim | Jeremiah 33:24 |

All point, in one way or another, to the House of Israel and the House of Judah. Referred to variously as Judah and Israel, Judah and Ephraim, House of Judah and House of Joseph, the pair tower at the center of scripture, with more prophecy about their destinies and reunification than about the Messiah! But, how? And, why?

*The central story in all of scripture*, and the central story in the prophesied 7,000 year history of Creation, occurs in the 11th and 12th chapters of 1 Kings. This account of the division of God's Covenant Nation vividly illustrates the blessings and prophecies spoken by Jacob over his sons Judah and Joseph. The division establishes the conditions for the drama to be resolved by the Redeemer-King who can fulfill the corporate needs of mankind while completing God's plan for a nation of priests.

Having seen the split between Judah and Ephraim, we must zoom out for a grand view of history to see that God had a plan and purpose for the division. As inexplicable as it was at the beginning, that plan is now considerably more visible with the passing of time. Each kingdom, the House of Israel and the House of Judah, had and has a different purpose and part of God's plan.

**The House of Israel**

Due to their chronic idolatry, God inflicted judgment on the House of Israel in the form of conquest by the Assyrian Empire. As with the death of any nation, the demise of Israel progressed over many years and many invasions. The final act, the siege of Israel's capital, Samaria, required three years to reach the inevitable conclusion in 721 BCE.

Israel's Northern Kingdom was but one of many nations that fell under Assyrian dominion. To maintain control over such a great number of diverse conquered peoples, the Assyrians practiced a system of assimilation, which involved taking 90% of each conquered population and resettling them in many places. This scattering of people groups proved effective in significantly reducing the chances of uprisings. The House of Israel was no exception; the Bible relates that they were resettled at the far corners of the Assyrian Empire – regions that correspond today to southeastern Turkey, northern Iraq, and northern Iran (2 Kings 17:6, 18:11-12, 1 Chronicles 5:26).

God repeatedly warned his people about the penalty for disobedience. In Leviticus 26, a chapter listing blessings for obedience and curses for disobedience, God promises,

> But if you do not obey Me and do not carry out all these commandments, if, instead, you reject My statutes, and if your soul abhors My ordinances so as not to carry out all My commandments, *and* so break My covenant, I, in turn, will do this to you: . . . I will make the land desolate so that your enemies who settle in it will be appalled over it. You, however, **I will scatter among the nations and will draw out a sword after you**, as your land becomes desolate and your cities become waste. (Leviticus 26:14-16, 32-33, emphasis added)

This judgment is confirmed in multiple other places with additional details, but with an accompanying message of hope. Two such examples occur in Deuteronomy, beginning in chapter 4:

> When you become the father of children and children's children and have remained long in the land, and act corruptly, and make an idol in the form of anything, and do that which is evil in the sight of the LORD your God *so as* to provoke Him to anger, I call heaven and earth to witness against you today, that you will surely perish quickly from the land where you are going over the Jordan to possess it. You shall not live long on it, but will be utterly destroyed. **The LORD will scatter you among the peoples**, and you will be left few in number among the nations where the LORD drives you. There you will serve gods, the work of man's hands, wood and stone, which neither see nor hear nor eat nor smell. **But from there you will seek the LORD your God, and you will find *Him* if you search for Him with all your heart and all your soul.** When you are in distress and all these things have come upon you, **in the latter days you will return to the LORD your God and listen to His voice**. For the LORD your God is a compassionate God; He will not fail you nor destroy you nor forget the covenant with your fathers which He swore to them. (Deuteronomy 4:25-31, emphasis added)

Deuteronomy 28 cites a similar judgment. In a fifty-verse warning, God concludes by saying:

> Moreover, **the LORD will scatter you among all peoples, from one end of the earth to the other end of the earth**; and there you shall serve other gods, wood and stone, which you or your fathers have not known. (Deuteronomy 28:64, emphasis added)

Yet the promise of restoration is clearly extended soon after this dire warning. Deuteronomy 30 begins with glorious verses promising that the scattered nation will be recovered and restored, a promise repeated over and over by the Prophets. In his final address, delivered just before Israel enters the Promised Land, Moses tells them:

> So it shall be when all of these things have come upon you, the blessing and the curse which I have set before you, and you call *them* to mind **in all nations where the LORD your God has banished you**, and you return to the LORD your God and obey Him with all your heart and soul according to all that I command you today, you and your sons, then **the LORD your God will restore you from captivity, and have compassion on you, and will gather you again from all the peoples where the LORD your God has scattered you**. <u>If your outcasts are at the ends of the earth, from there the LORD your God will gather you, and from there He will bring you back. The LORD your God will bring you into the land which your fathers possessed, and you shall possess it; and He will prosper you and multiply you more than your fathers</u>. Moreover the LORD your God will circumcise your heart and the heart of your descendants, to love the LORD your God with all your heart and with all your soul, so that you may live. (Deuteronomy 30:1-6, emphasis added)

The scattering and the regathering were clearly part of God's plan from the very beginning. With the hindsight of history, we can see that, while both Houses have been scattered, the application of that lot has fallen more heavily on the House of Israel. While a desperate fate, it was a fate with a purpose.

As we shall see, the Apostles understood this aspect of the House of Israel. They understood as well that a primary component of the Gospel of the Kingdom was restoration to the Covenant of those who had been scattered and banished. The Messiah made a way of return. What the Apostles may not have anticipated, however, was the length of the sentence of exile.

In Ezekiel 4, we read that the prophet was commanded to lie on his left side for the iniquity of the House of Israel. The text says:

> As for you, lie down on your left side and lay the iniquity of the house of Israel on it; you shall bear their iniquity for the number of days that you lie on it. **For I have assigned you a number of days corresponding to the years of their iniquity, three hundred and ninety days**; thus you shall bear the iniquity of the house of Israel. (Ezekiel 4:4-5, emphasis added)

Ezekiel recorded this prophecy over a hundred years after the Assyrian conquest of Samaria, and about six hundred years before the Apostles began preaching the Gospel of the Kingdom. Nearly twice the specified time period of 390 years had elapsed, but the exiles had not yet returned. Was Ezekiel mistaken, or was there another factor at work? Perhaps another witness from scripture that, when understood, would indicate a considerably longer exile?

Previously, I quoted Leviticus 26:33, which refers to the scattering of the people for disobedience. The scattering would happen as the culmination of a series of progressive judgments inflicted for continued disobedience. But that is not all. In addition to adding judgments, the intensity and length of each judgment would be increased sevenfold if the people refused to repent. Four times in that chapter, the Lord explains he will "punish you seven times for your sins" (Leviticus 26:18, 21, 24, 28). In the case of the exile, it would be multiplication of the number of years by a factor of seven.

Now let us do some math:

$$390 \text{ years} \times 7\text{-fold punishment} = 2{,}730 \text{ years}$$

Does history reveal any correlation to this time period? Perhaps. Remember that the exile of the House of Israel began about 721 BCE. There is no "year 0" between the BCE and CE eras, which means the arithmetic is straightforward:

721 BCE + 2730 years = 2009 CE

While this date is significant, it is not within the scope of this book to explain the details. In brief, as we see in Deuteronomy 30, God promises to regather his people who had been scattered when "you return to the LORD your God and obey him with all your heart and soul according to all that I command you today." (Deuteronomy 30:2) The return of the exiles is connected to a return to obedience to the Torah of Moses, a phenomenon seen across the planet throughout Christian circles in recent years. This is exactly in keeping with the instructions in the last chapter of Malachi regarding the latter days:

> Remember the law [Torah] of Moses My servant, ***even the statutes and ordinances which I commanded him in Horeb for all Israel***. Behold, I am going to send you Elijah the prophet before the coming of the great and terrible day of the LORD. He will restore the hearts of the fathers to *their* children and the hearts of the children to their fathers, so that I will not come and smite the land with a curse. (Malachi 4:4-6, emphasis added)

Micah 4 and Isaiah 2 provide additional testimony, both stating nearly verbatim:

> And it will come about in the last days that the mountain of the house of the LORD will be established as the chief of the mountains. It will be raised above the hills, and the peoples will stream to it. Many nations will come and say, "Come and let us go up to the mountain of the LORD and to the house of the God of Jacob, **that He may teach us about His ways** and that we may walk in His paths." **For from Zion will go forth the law [Torah]**, even the word of the LORD from Jerusalem. (Micah 4:1-2, Isaiah 2:2-4, emphasis added)

As we will see, the Apostles recognized that one of the major roles of the Messiah was to be a Redeemer who would make the way for the "lost sheep of the House of Israel" (Matthew 10:5-7, 15:24) to come back into covenant with the God of Abraham, Isaac, and Jacob. Here we begin to understand the role of the House of Israel in this great drama of restoration that reveals the mysterious and unfathomable ways of our God. Not only will the "lost sheep" be restored to the Covenant and the Torah of the Almighty, but they will bring with them multitudes from every nation in which they have been scattered over the centuries!

The House of Israel was that portion of the seed of Abraham, Isaac, and Jacob destined to be scattered to the ends of the earth, and then, through the Messiah, bring forth fruit – even though they did not fully understand or remember who they were. Essentially, the House of Israel and those gathered to them have been leaven for the Kingdom, taking the message of the Messiah to the ends of the earth. Now, having done so, we are being awakened to the fullness of our identity as members of the commonwealth of Israel according to what Paul says in Ephesians 2:

> Therefore remember that formerly you, the Gentiles in the flesh, who are called "Uncircumcision" by the so-called "Circumcision," *which is* performed in the flesh by human hands—*remember* that you were at that time separate from Christ, excluded from the **commonwealth of Israel**, and strangers to the covenants of promise, having no hope and without God in the world. But now in Christ Jesus you who formerly were far off have been brought near by the blood of Christ. (Ephesians 2:11-13, emphasis added)

The House of Israel has been a witness throughout the world to the eternal mercy of God and his Messiah. The witness given by the House of Judah has been no less profound, but quite different.

## The House of Judah

Judah, like the Northern Kingdom of Israel, fell into idolatry and judgment, resulting in their exile to Babylon. As with the Assyrian conquest of Israel, the Babylonian conquest of Judah proceeded in stages over many years, culminating with the destruction of Jerusalem and the Temple of the Lord in 586 BCE. Unlike the Assyrians, the Babylonians did not scatter the Jews. Instead, they resettled the Jews in communities in Mesopotamia (modern day Iraq) where they retained their identity and began to consider carefully their need to be obedient to the Father's Torah. As the Lord promised through Jeremiah (Jeremiah 25:11-12, 29:10), after 70 years many returned and rebuilt the Temple. Ezra and Nehemiah recount this return.

Although the House of Judah did gain a degree of independence under the Hasmonean kings of the $2^{nd}$ and $1^{st}$ centuries BCE, they never regained the status of former days when a son of David reigned in Jerusalem. Even during that period of independence, the Jewish nation was subject to the dictates of the powerful empires which Daniel had prophesied would dominate them: Babylon, Persia, Greece, and Rome.

Independence, though, was not the primary role assigned to Judah. Their role was to bring forth the Messiah from the House of David, according to prophecy, and to protect the Torah through the ages. Paul testifies to this vital role in his letter to Rome:

> Then what advantage has the Jew? Or what is the benefit of circumcision? Great in every respect. First of all, that they were entrusted with the oracles of God. (Romans 3:1-2)

The House of Judah accomplished well the role the Father gave them, though not without much pain and suffering. Persecuted and pursued through history – by the church as much as by any other group – the Jews have paid a heavy price for guarding the Torah.

After their return to Babylon, the Jewish nation endured oppression under multiple foreign rulers. Following the death of Alexander the Great and the dissolution of his empire, the Jews found themselves initially under the Egyptian Ptolemaic Kingdom before falling to the Hellenistic Seleucids in about 200 BCE. Internal struggle ensued as the Seleucid Greeks under Antiochus IV Epiphanes (r. 175-164 BCE) applied intense pressure to erase all worship of YHVH and obedience to his Torah, and replace it with the appealing, but worldly, Hellenistic culture. At the height of his persecution of the Jews, Antiochus abolished Shabbat and observance of the Feasts of the Lord, and desecrated the Temple. Although many Jews either cooperated with or succumbed to the Hellenistic onslaught, a small band of pious Jews led by the family of the Maccabees waged a guerilla war that resulted in the miraculous defeat of Antiochus' forces and the rededication of the Temple.

The Hasmonean Dynasty of priest-kings established by the Maccabees soon fell under the influence of a new imperial overlord: Rome. In 37 BCE, the Romans placed their client, Herod, on the throne of Judea, cementing their control over the Jewish nation. Control, that is; not peace. The Jews chafed under Roman domination, and after multiple revolts and rebellions, the Roman legions waged a war of annihilation that resulted in destruction of the Temple in 70 CE. One generation later, a second and even more disastrous war took place in response to the Bar Kokhba Rebellion of 135 CE. When it was all over, the Romans had killed or enslaved millions of Jews, and anti-Semitism became the cultural and legal norm in every corner of the Empire.

That anti-Semitism accelerated a trend that had begun even in the first century as Gentiles and non-Jewish followers of Messiah Yeshua increasingly distanced themselves from Jews. At the beginning, Christians of all backgrounds attended the synagogues, worshipping alongside Jews, or at least observed the Sabbath and maintained the instructions of the Jewish Apostles (Acts 15:13-21). That began to change as more and more non-Jews responded favorably to the message of redemption through Yeshua. As their numbers grew far beyond those of their Jewish brethren, and as succeeding generations became removed in time from the Hebraic outlook of the first believers, the great Roman-Jewish wars merely ensured that the separation would become the norm.

The decrees of Caesar Hadrian, who expelled Jews from Jerusalem and renamed Judea "Syria Palaestina" (the origin of the term, "Palestine"), made anti-Semitism an imperial policy, establishing a precedent that later Caesars and Christian bishops in Rome would perpetuate. By the time Constantine the Great declared the Empire to be Christian early in the 4th Century, Christianity was already well on the way toward becoming a separate religion from Judaism. Constantine's religious policies provided legal grounds for erasing most of the remaining Hebrew roots from what became the Church of Rome and its daughters in Western Christianity. As the centuries progressed, the animosity against Jews and everything Jewish led to expulsions from country after country in Europe, innumerable pogroms, official persecution in the form of the Inquisition, and even the gas chambers and ovens of Nazi Germany's death camps.

In spite of the horrors, the Jews have always been a recognizable people who kept the Sabbath and the Feasts of the Lord, have eaten according to the Bible's dietary laws, and are easily identified by their set-apart dress. Today, against all odds, they are reestablished in the Land and flourishing as a visible testimony to God's eternal Covenant and his blessing to those who remain faithfully obedient to his Torah.

The House of Judah has been a witness throughout the world to the covenant faithfulness of God and his Torah.

## Two Witnesses

Scripture depicts the House of Israel and the House of Judah as two witnesses in many, many ways. Returning to those listed at the beginning of this chapter, we can begin to see how the pictures fit both Houses, particularly when we understand that much of the House of Israel is embedded within the church:

| House of Judah | House of Israel |
|---|---|
| Stick of Judah | Stick of Joseph/Ephraim |
| Moses (House of Judah) | Elijah (Tishbite, *ger*?)[1] |
| Law/Torah | Prophets |
| Truth | Spirit |
| Caleb (Tribe of Judah) | Joshua (Tribe of Ephraim) |
| Elder Brother | Prodigal Son |
| Written Word | Living Word |

---

[1] *Ger*, (גּוּר, Strongs #H1481) is often translated as stranger, alien, or foreigner. Scripture does not tell us much about Elijah's identity. He may have been from Tishbe, a town in the Gilead portion of Manasseh east of the Jordan, and thus a Manassite. However, it is possible that he may have been a foreigner (*ger*) who lived in Israel.

It is interesting to note that in the closing chapter of the Christian Old Testament (Malachi is ordered differently in the Jewish Bible) we find the mention of both Moses and Elijah. In six very rich and decidedly eschatological verses we are instructed to:

> Remember the law [Torah] of Moses My servant, *even the* statutes and ordinances which I commanded him in Horeb for all Israel.
> Behold, I am going to send you Elijah the prophet before the coming of the great and terrible day of the LORD. He will restore the hearts of the fathers to *their* children and the hearts of the children to their fathers, so that I will not come and smite the land with a curse. (Malachi 4:4-6)

A common Christian interpretation is that these two, Moses and Elijah, are the two witnesses spoken of in Revelation 11. Notice, however, that John gives a couple of other details as to who the witnesses are, drawing from Zechariah:

> "And I will grant *authority* to my **two witnesses**, and they will prophesy for twelve hundred and sixty days, clothed in sackcloth." These are the **two olive trees** and the **two lampstands** that stand before the Lord of the earth. (Revelation 11:3-4, emphasis added)

Zechariah 4 has this to say:

> He said to me, "What do you see?" And I said, "I see, and behold, a lampstand all of gold with its bowl on the top of it, and its seven lamps on it with seven spouts belonging to each of the lamps which are on the top of it; also **two olive trees** by it, one on the right side of the bowl and the other on its left side."
> Then I said to him, "What are these **two olive trees** on the right of the lampstand and on its left?" And I answered the second time and said to him, **"What are the two olive branches which are beside the two golden pipes, which empty the golden *oil* from themselves?"** So he answered me, saying, "Do you not know what these are?" And I said, "No, my lord." Then he said, "These are the **two anointed**

**ones** who are standing by the Lord of the whole earth." (Zechariah 4:2-3, 11-14, emphasis added)

Note that "anointed ones" is literally translated, "sons of fresh oil," a phrase pointing directly to the New Covenant. Note also that nowhere in scripture is an individual ever called an "olive tree," but we do see Jeremiah using the Hebrew word for olive tree that Zechariah uses (*zayith*, זַיִת, Strongs #H2132) when speaking to the House of Israel and the House of Judah:

> The LORD called your name, "A **green olive tree**, beautiful in fruit and form"; with the noise of a great tumult He has kindled fire on it, and its branches are worthless. (Jeremiah 11:16, emphasis added)

Hosea echoes this same name of "olive tree" in a final promise to Ephraim/Israel:

> His shoots will sprout, and his beauty will be like the **olive tree** and his fragrance like *the cedars of* Lebanon. (Hosea 14:6, emphasis added)

Paul picks up this motif in Romans 11 regarding the restoration of the Kingdom. Ezekiel pursues the same motif, but uses a slightly different word. When speaking of the two sticks, Ezekiel uses the word *etz* (עֵץ, Strongs #H6086), which can mean stick or tree.

Another way to visualize all these passages is through the imagery of the *menorah* (מְנוֹרָה, Strongs #H4501), sometimes translated as lampstand or candlestick. The menorah is a special type of candlestick that can be described as a form of tree with multiple branches.

Two candlesticks –

Two trees –

**TWO WITNESSES**

## AN ANCIENT NEAR EAST SUPERPOWER

Kings David and Solomon presided over a united kingdom of Israel that projected power from Egypt to Mesopotamia, but Israel's golden age lasted less than a century. Tribal jealousies divided the kingdom soon after Solomon's death.

Hurlbut, *Bible Atlas*, 68.

# 5

# THE RABBIS WERE RIGHT

**A People Still Scattered**

A common objection to the Two House position is that it is in error because the House of Israel, the "ten Lost Tribes," have already returned. That objection is partially correct. Scripture does attest that *elements* of the tribes returned, but the consistent witness of scripture and history is that the prophesied return of uncounted multitudes is yet to be realized. We have already encountered Hosea's word on this subject:

> **Yet the number of the sons of Israel will be like the sand of the sea, which cannot be measured or numbered**; and in the place where it is said to them, "You are not My people," it will be said to them, "*You are* the sons of the living God." And the sons of Judah and the sons of Israel will be gathered together, and they will appoint for themselves one leader, and they will go up from the land, for great will be the day of Jezreel. (Hosea 1:10-11, emphasis added)

God's promise states plainly that the numbers of returning Israelites will be something of incredible magnitude. Further, this passage articulates that the prophecy is specifically for those called "not My people," meaning the House of Israel. To understand that Hosea is addressing the House of Israel when he speaks to the "sons of Israel," one has only to look at this passage in context. After establishing that his prophetic career occurred during the reign of Jeroboam II of Israel (c. 789-748 BCE), Hosea writes:

> When the LORD first spoke through Hosea, the LORD said to Hosea, "Go, take to yourself a wife of harlotry and *have* children of harlotry; for the land commits flagrant harlotry, forsaking the LORD." So he went and took Gomer the

daughter of Diblaim, and she conceived and bore him a son. And the LORD said to him, "Name him Jezreel [God Sows, or God Scatters]; for yet a little while, and I will punish the house of Jehu for the bloodshed of Jezreel, and I will put an end to the kingdom of the house of Israel. On that day I will break the bow of Israel in the valley of Jezreel."
Then she conceived again and gave birth to a daughter. And the LORD said to him, "Name her Lo-ruhamah [No Mercy], for I will no longer have compassion on the house of Israel, that I would ever forgive them. But I will have compassion on the house of Judah and deliver them by the LORD their God, and will not deliver them by bow, sword, battle, horses or horsemen."
When she had weaned Lo-ruhamah, she conceived and gave birth to a son. And the LORD said, "Name him Lo-ammi [Not My People], for you are not My people and I am not your God." (Hosea 1:2-5)

As we have seen, the prophet makes a clear distinction here between the judgments to be visited upon the House of Israel and the House of Judah. Since he is a prophet to the Northern Kingdom (an assignment he shares with his contemporaries Jonah, Amos, and Micah), Hosea provides more detail about what will happen to Israel than he relates concerning Judah. (See Isaiah, Jeremiah, and Ezekiel for the details about Judah's judgment.) In these verses in his opening chapter, Hosea foretells a progression of judgment through the names of his children. The first, Jezreel, is aimed at the ruling dynasty which began with Jehu and will end with Zechariah, son of Jeroboam II. Hosea specifically references the bloody deed of Jehu when he seized the throne and slaughtered the descendants of King Ahab at Jezreel (2 Kings 9:1-10:11).

Jehu had done as YHVH commanded by eradicating Ahab's house, but he failed to lead Israel in repentance and a return to the Torah. Therefore the Lord promised that his dynasty would last only four generations (2 Kings 10:28-31). Jeroboam II was the third generation of kings from the House of Jehu, and one of the most powerful and prosperous of the Northern Kingdom's monarchs. It would have been inconceivable at the time that Hosea and his contemporaries would speak of an imminent end not only of Jehu's dynasty, but also of the House of Israel altogether. And yet, within one generation, it had come to pass, just as the names of Hosea's second and third children proclaimed.

Hosea does not end there. In chapter 3 we learn something of what will happen to these same sons of Israel after their destruction as a nation:

> Then the LORD said to me, "Go again, love a woman *who* is loved by *her* husband, yet an adulteress, even as the LORD loves the sons of Israel, though they turn to other gods and love raisin cakes." So I bought her for myself for fifteen *shekels* of silver and a homer and a half of barley. Then I said to her, "You shall stay with me for many days. You shall not play the harlot, nor shall you have a man; so I will also be toward you." **For the sons of Israel will remain for many days without king or prince, without sacrifice or *sacred* pillar and without ephod or household idols. Afterward the sons of Israel will return and seek the LORD their God and David their king; and they will come trembling to the LORD and to His goodness in the last days.** (Hosea 3:1-5, emphasis added)

Here the prophet goes back even further in time, to the point at which the House of Israel divided itself from the House of Judah with the declaration:

> "What portion do we have in David? *We have* no inheritance in the son of Jesse; to your tents, O Israel! Now look after your own house, David!" (1 Kings 12:16)

Judah was by no means perfect, but the Jewish nation did remain loyal to the line of David and to the God who anointed David and his descendants as rulers of all Israel (1 Kings 1:1-14; 2 Samuel 7:8-15; Jeremiah 33:19-22). When the northern tribes cut their ties with David's dynasty, they cut their ties as well to David's capital, Jerusalem, and to David's God. The new order they established encompassed every aspect of the political, spiritual, economic, and social order, in effect duplicating on a national scale the original sin of Adam and Eve by becoming gods unto themselves. Thus the judgment pronounced in Hosea chapter 3 involved removal of every aspect of that political, spiritual, economic, and social life. To understand what was lost, consider this list of the Covenant Nation's attributes that Paul shares in connection with the Jewish people:

> For I could wish that I myself were accursed, *separated* from Christ for the sake of my brethren, my kinsmen according to the flesh, who are Israelites, to whom belongs the adoption as sons, and the glory and the covenants and the giving of the Law and the *temple* service and the promises, whose are the fathers, and from whom is the Christ according to the flesh, who is over all, God blessed forever. Amen. (Romans 9:3-5)

It is a testimony to the mercy of the Lord that the House of Judah retained these blessings so they could carry out their destiny as a witness for the Holy One. However, this list provides a sobering realization of the enormity of Ephraim's loss. As severe as the judgment inflicted on the Jewish nation for their rebellion, nothing quite compares to the total death of the northern Israelite nation – a death which has not been reversed even to this day, although it is clearly promised.

Interestingly, we see this national death of Ephraim referenced by the Apostle Paul in his explanation of Messiah Yeshua's work of redemption. Specifically, Paul refers to this passage of Hosea's prophecy:

> The iniquity of Ephraim is bound up; his sin is stored up. The pains of childbirth come upon him; he is not a wise son, for it is not the time that he should delay at the opening of the womb. Shall I ransom them from the power of Sheol? Shall I redeem them from death? **O Death, where are your thorns? O Sheol, where is your sting?** Compassion will be hidden from My sight. (Hosea 13:12-14, emphasis added)

Paul draws on Hosea to make his point in one of the most familiar sections of his own writings:

> Now I say this, brethren, that flesh and blood cannot inherit the kingdom of God; nor does the perishable inherit the imperishable. Behold, I tell you a mystery; we will not all sleep, but we will all be changed, in a moment, in the

twinkling of an eye, at the last trumpet; for the trumpet will sound, and the dead will be raised imperishable, and we will be changed. For this perishable must put on the imperishable, and this mortal must put on immortality. But when this perishable will have put on the imperishable, and this mortal will have put on immortality, then will come about the saying that is written, "DEATH IS SWALLOWED UP in victory. **O DEATH, WHERE IS YOUR VICTORY? O DEATH, WHERE IS YOUR STING?**" The sting of death is sin, and the power of sin is the law; but thanks be to God, who gives us the victory through our Lord Jesus Christ. (1 Corinthians 15:50-57, emphasis added)

For centuries, this passage has served as a foundational reference for the Christian understanding of personal salvation and resurrection offered through faith in Messiah Yeshua. As with so much of church teaching, that is correct, but a greater dimension of meaning unfolds when we see the linkage with Hosea. Does this mean that the Apostle Paul, and perhaps the other Apostles, connected Yeshua's redemptive work with the return of the Lost Tribes? Since the original Apostles were all Jewish, any expectations they may have had regarding the Lost Tribes would have been informed by Jewish understanding of the day.

## Rabbinic Expectations

A persistent expectation among Jewish Rabbis is the connection of Messiah with the Lost Tribes. Proof of Messiah's coming will be that he either brings the Lost Tribes with him, or reveals where they can be found. Without question, the rabbis have understood that the House of Israel is distinct from the House of Judah, and is destined to return at the end of the age.

The writings of the Jewish Sages are peppered with commentary on the disposition and whereabouts of the Ten Tribes. Chief among the quotes is a discussion between Rabbi Aqiba and Rabbi Eliezer held in the generation after the destruction of the Second Temple in 70 CE. Their discussion, cited in the Talmud, Tractate Sanhedrin 11:3, sets the tone for the Rabbinic discussion:

> The ten tribes who were exiled will not be returned, as it reads [Deut. xxix 27]: "And he cast them into another land, as this day." As that day will not return, so will they not return. So R. Aqiba.
>
> R. Eliezer said: As this day means as usually a day becomes clouded and thereafter lights up again, so the ten tribes, who are now in darkness, the future will lighten upon them.[1]

In several other places, Rabbi Aqiba is quoted as agreeing with the position of Eliezer, although Aqiba is largely considered the main voice for the minority position of a non-return.

Second Temple Judaism's expectation is demonstrated by the last and apparently most burning question the disciples asked of Yeshua before his departure:

> So when they had come together, they were asking Him, saying, **"Lord, is it at this time You are restoring the kingdom to Israel?"** He said to them, "It is not for you to know times or epochs which the Father has fixed by His own authority; but you will receive power when the Holy Spirit has come upon you; and you shall be My witnesses both in Jerusalem, and in all Judea and Samaria, and even to the remotest part of the earth." (Acts 1:6-8, emphasis added)

Why would the Apostles ask such a question if they did not expect Messiah to restore the Kingdom to Israel? And what did "restoring the kingdom" mean to them? I will explore the answers to those questions in more detail later. For now, merely note that the Apostles, like the rabbis, expected Messiah to restore the entire Kingdom to Israel. It is clear that they, too, expected Messiah to bring back the Lost Tribes.

The best case for this rabbinic understanding is made by Nachmanides, or the Ramban, as Rabbi Moshe ben Nachman

---

[1] *The Babylonian Talmud: Tract Sanhedrin*, trans. Michael L. Rodkinson (Boston: The Talmud Society, 1918), accessed October 25, 2017, https://archive.org/stream/TheBabylonianTalmudVols1-1--MichaelL.Rodkinson/TheBabylonianTalmud-Book8-Vols.XvXvi-Tr.ByMichaelL.Rodkinson1918#page/n287/mode/2up.

(1194-1270) is more popularly known. The Ramban was a prolific thinker and writer, and is regarded as one of Judaism's greatest theological minds. Among his writings is *Sefer HaGeulah*, the *Scroll of Redemption*. The Ramban makes a solid case not only that the Northern Kingdom never came home, but that there will be a redemption in the latter days. He articulates from Ezra, Nehemiah and the Chronicles a foundation that concludes:

> Now, we have not made any novel points in this subject other than to present scattered verses. Nevertheless, from our words it has been explained that in the redemption from Babylon, only those who were called "the House of Yehudah" returned [to the Land], and this was their kingdom [during the Second Temple]. However, those who were called "the House of Efraim" or "the House of Israel," comprising the ten tribes, did remain in the Assyrian captivity to this day. No ensign [of deliverance] was raised for their tribes, and there was none that escaped during this redemption, as we have mentioned.[2]

The Ramban continues with a short discussion of Obadiah, verse 11:

> Additionally, there is *The vision of Ovadiah* {Obadiah}, which is necessarily a prophet for [a period] subsequent to the Babylonian captivity in Jerusalem, as it is written, *In the day that you* [Edom] *stood aloof, in the day that strangers carried away his substance, and foreigners entered into his gates, and cast lots upon Jerusalem,* and [so on through] the entire subject. Afterwards, it says, *And the house of Yaakov* {Jacob} *shall be afire, and the house of Yosef aflame, and the house of Eisav* {Esau} *for stubble, and they shall kindle in them, and devour them, and there shall not be any remaining of the house of Eisav.* Scholars who say this prophecy concerned the days of Chizkiyah {Hezekiah} or [the period of] Second Temple are *a people that err in their heart.*[3]

---

[2] Ramban Nachmanides, *Writings of the Ramban*, Revised Ed., vol. 2, trans. Rabbi Charles B. Chavel (Brooklyn, NY: Shilo Publishing House, 2009), 649.
[3] Ibid, 651.

In continuing his sharp critique, the Ramban maintains a firm position that the ten tribes are still in exile:

> It is a known fact that in Scripture, this name, *the house of Yosef* {Joseph}, relates to the kingdom of Israel, which was composed of the ten tribes, [which did not return from their exile in Assyria since the days of Chizkiyah]. Why should these [scholars] not be ashamed of [their interpretation in light of] this [last] verse quoted, for when *the house of Yosef [aflame]* upon *the house of Eisav for stubble*? [The ten tribes] were long ago taken into exile and are still there. These are the exiles of Zarefas and Canaan, which are at the northern ends. . . . The ascension from Babylon began in the days of Ezra, as has been explained to you, and these distant ones, [that is, the ten tribes exiled in Assyria], did not come *as the doves to their windows.*[4]

The Ramban's writings are a major guiding influence for modern Orthodox Jewish thought. Simply put, the return has not happened, but prophecy promises that it will. Moreover, the return is regarded as <u>the</u> *sign of the Messiah*, who will regather the scattered of Israel.

Rabbinic thought varies as to how this return will occur and how "Jewish" the exiles will look. For many centuries, the expectation was that the tribes would be found intact behind some mountain or across some river. Fabled legends developed involving mystical accounts of the tribes being across a river called the Sambatyon, a river not of water, but of rough flowing sand and debris that ran six days per week and rested on the Sabbath. While fantastic in its detail, the tales illustrate the seeming hopelessness of the situation and the utter disappearance of the tribes, save the scant fragments that joined with Judah either at the original division of the Kingdom, or upon the destruction of Samaria.

It was this desire to know the whereabouts of the tribes that drove a number of global explorations. Christopher Columbus, himself a Jew, left notes in Hebrew in the margins of his journal that indicate this very search may have been a motivation for his multiple trips to the New World. Famed Nazi hunter Simon Wiesenthal confirms

---

[4] Ibid., 651-652.

this in his well-researched book on the topic, *Sails of Hope: The Secret Mission of Christopher Columbus*. He says, "It is necessary, therefore, to go back a bit in history, first, because nowadays too little is known about the search for the lost tribes of Israel, and secondly, because in my opinion this matter is intimately bound up with the venture of Christopher Columbus."[5]

Wiesenthal continues, "At any rate by the ninth century it was an article of faith, not only among the Jews but *among the Christian population*, that the ten lost tribes did exist somewhere outside the borders of the known world."[6] In recent centuries, Christians abandoned belief in the future return of the ten lost tribes largely, in our opinion, because theologians ceased to understand hard prophecies in a literal way. Instead, prophecies that did not comport with Christian theology began to be ignored or spiritualized in a way that they would make sense within the Christian paradigm.

The House of Judah has never given up an expectation of the return of the ten lost tribes. However, their understandings and expectations have had to shift a bit. As global exploration drew to a close without the discovery of any intact Israelite tribes, the Jewish search adjusted to looking for cultural clues that might identify people groups with some Hebraic heritage.[7] One leading organization dedicated to finding traces of the lost tribes is Amishav, founded in 1975 by Ravbbi Eliyahu Avichail. He "has travelled the world, from India, Burma, China, Thailand and Japan to Europe and South America, in order to research, encourage and guide the dispersed of Israel." Shavei Israel is another organization

---

[5] Simon Wiesenthal, *Sails of Hope: The Secret Mission of Christopher Columbus*, trans. Richard and Clara Winston (New York: MacMillan, 1973), 61.
[6] Ibid., 61, emphasis added.
[7] I am careful to specify "Hebraic" rather than "Jewish" heritage. Although the primary search for the Lost Tribes has been by Jews seeking what are believed to be "Jewish" tribes, the fact is these exiles were never Jewish. The tell-tale cultural traits have come to be identified as "Jewish" simply because the only identifiable cultural expression of the Hebrew nation since 721 BCE has been Jewish. Jewish cultural expression is the best (and only) starting point for identifying lost Hebrew people groups, but it is not consistent with Scripture or the record of history to assume that the Lost Tribes ever were or ever will be Jewish.

that was founded in 2002 by a former director of Amishav. Even the Israeli government has had a recent undertaking in research to measure and consider the possible avenues for repatriation of the Spanish *Conversos*, or forced converts who fled Spain in the late 1400s and early 1500s to find refuge in Central and South America.[8]

Many genetically and culturally connected lost Hebrews have indeed been found, such as the Bnei Menashe, Bnei Ephraim, and Mizo peoples of India and Myanmar (Burma),[9] the Pathan (Pashtun) of Afghanistan and Pakistan,[10] and the Lemba and Igbo of Africa.[11] Others include the Kurdish people of Iraq, Turkey,

---

[8] "Rabbi Eliyahu Avichail," *Amishav*, accessed July 12, 2017, http://amishav-onetree.org/53-2/; "Communities," *Shavei Israel*, accessed July 12, 2017, https://shavei.org/communities/; Rabbi Mendy Elishevitz, "Will the Lost 10 Tribes Return?," *Moshiach.com*, updated November 25, 2003, accessed July 12, 2017, http://beta.moshiach.com/index.php/item/will-the-lost-10-tribes-return; "Circles of the Jewish People," Israel Ministry of Diaspora Affairs, accessed July 12, 2017, http://www.mda.gov.il/EngSite/Diaspora/Pages/Circles.aspx.

[9] "The Bnei Menashe of India," *Bnei Menashe: Lost Tribe Coming Home*, accessed July 12, 2017, http://www.bneimenashe.com/; Margot Crossing, "Home B'nai Menashe from Mizoram," *Lost Tribes Found Blog*, November 9, 2015, accessed October 19, 2017, https://losttribesfoundblog.wordpress.com/2015/11/09/home-bnai-menashe-from-mizoram/; Margot Crossing, "Hill Tribe Peoples of the Lost Book," *Lost Tribes Found Blog*, November 9, 2015, accessed October 19, 2017, https://losttribesfoundblog.wordpress.com/2015/11/09/hill-tribe-peoples-of-the-lost-book/; Margot Crossing, "What is the Difference Between These and the B'ney Menashe?," *Lost Tribes Found Blog*, October 20, 2017, accessed October 20, 2017, https://losttribesfoundblog.wordpress.com/2017/10/20/what-is-the-difference-between-these-and-the-bnei-menashe/.

[10] Rory McCarthy, "Pashtun clue to lost tribes of Israel," *The Guardian*, January 16, 2010, accessed October 25, 2017, http://www.theguardian.com/world/2010/jan/17/israel-lost-tribes-pashtun; Ari Z. Zivotofsky and Ari Greenspan, "Pashtun Pride, Israel Denied," *Jewish World Review*, May 6, 2015, accessed July 12, 2017, http://www.jewishworldreview.com/0515/pashtun_jews.php3.

[11] Rabbi Yehudah "Tochukwu" ben Shomeyr, "The Lemba," *Hebrew Igbo*, accessed July 12, 2017, http://www.hebrewigbo.com/lemba.html; Rabbi Yehudah "Tochukwu" ben Shomeyr, "Am I Afraid," *Hebrew Igbo*, accessed July 12, 2017, http://www.hebrewigbo.com/israel-igbo.html; Samuel Kurinsky, "Jews in Africa," Fact Papers 19-I 19-II, 19-III, and 19-IV, *Hebrew History Foundation*, accessed July 12, 2017,

Syria, and Iran, who still live in the regions where the Assyrian Empire exiled the Israelite tribes over 2,700 years ago. [12] Moreover, the connection of Native American or First Nations tribes with the Lost Tribes of Israel has been understood since the earliest days of European exploration of the Americas.[13] In fact, there are those who claim that the peoples of Europe and the British Isles are at least partially descended from ancient Israel.[14] And, of course, there are still millions of "hidden Jews," or *Anusim*, throughout the world, particularly the Americas. Often

---

http://www.hebrewhistory.info/factpapers.htm.

[12] M.R. Izady, "Are Kurds Descended from the Medes?," *Kurdish Life*, No. 10 (1994), accessed July 12, 2017, http://www.kurdistanica.com/?q=node/32; Kendal Nezan, "A Brief Survey of the History of the Kurds," *Fondation Institut Kurde de Paris*, accessed July 12, 2017, http://www.institutkurde.org/en/institute/who_are_the_kurds.php; Mehrdad R. Izady, "Judaism," *The Kurds, A Concise Handbook*, (Harvard: 1992), accessed July 12, 2017, http://www.kurdistanica.com/?q=node/105.

[13] David Koffman, "Native Americans and Jews: The Lost Tribes Episode, An all-too forgotten historical debate," *My Jewish Learning*, accessed July 12, 2017, http://www.myjewishlearning.com/article/native-americans-jews-the-lost-tribes-episode/; Akiva Levitas, "The lost tribes: Bringing the Jewish and Aboriginal communities closer together," *The Nation*, December 19, 2013, accessed July 12, 2017, http://www.nationnews.ca/the-lost-tribes-bringing-the-jewish-and-aboriginal-communities-closer-together/; Adam Eliyahu Berkowitz, "Are Native Americans Part of the Ten Lost Tribes?," *Breaking Israel News*, October 25, 2016, accessed October 25, 2017, https://www.breakingisraelnews.com/77499/native-americans-part-ten-lost-tribes/#hOFSixswBQrcZez0.97.

[14] The mystery of the Ten Lost Tribes is a subject that has remained on the fringes of "respectable" scholarship. Serious, credentialed scholars have done creditable research in archaeology, linguistics, anthropology, genetics, history, and other disciplines in an effort to trace the Ten Tribes through history and identify their descendants today. This research has turned up a consistent body of evidence indicating various places to which the descendants of Israel and of Judah migrated after the ancient conquests by Assyria and Babylon. Those interested in investigating and judging these things could start by reviewing the work of Yair Davidiy, Steven M. Collins, and Drs. Alex and Georgina Perdomo. Yair Davidiy, *Brit-Am, Movement of the Ten Tribes of Israel*, accessed July 12, 2017, http://britam.org/; Yair Davidiy, *Hebrew Nations: A Britam Website*, accessed July 12, 2017, http://hebrewnations.com/; Steven M. Collins, *Steven M. Collins*, accessed October 19, 2017, http://stevenmcollins.com/; Alex and Georgina Perdomo, *Etz Yosef Project*, accessed July 12, 2017, http://etzyoseph.org/.

known as *Conversos* or *Marranos*, these are the descendants of Jews forced to convert to Christianity or other faiths, but who "clandestinely cherished their Jewish faith." Combined, these people groups number in the millions, but it seems the prophecies attest to a far greater number even than these.

Multiple places in scripture point to an innumerable host returning to the Land. We can infer from this that those people groups identified as Hebraic through their cultural traits only partially fit the prophecies. For example, one prophecy by Zechariah, when "reverse engineered," gives a clue as to the size of the returning remnant:

> Thus says the LORD of hosts, "In those days ten men from all the nations will grasp the garment of a Jew, saying, 'Let us go with you, for we have heard that God is with you.'" (Zechariah 8:23)

There are over 6 million Jews in Israel today. If we multiply that number by 10, the returning remnant would be 60,000,000 souls joining themselves to Judah.

The global Jewish population is over 14 million Jews, placing a possible remnant at closer to 140,000,000 who attach themselves to Judah.

But does this mean they are to become Jewish? My understanding is no; these returning Hebrews do come back to Torah, but they retain the distinction of their own House as they join with the Jewish people to complete the nation. In fact, it is my understanding that many of the exiles are coming not from distinct ethnic or tribal groups, but from within Christianity. Therefore, if we consider a 10% remnant of all Christendom, estimated at 2 billion worldwide, then the remnant of returning Israelites would be close to 200 million!

With numbers so large, it is no wonder that even modern rabbis question how such a fulfillment is possible when there are no cultures or peoples who fit the expected "Jewish look." This in itself is a reflection of the prevailing notion that Israel consists entirely of the Jewish people.

Exceptions to that prevailing notion have been few, but they are becoming more numerous. One of them is Hanoch Young, an American-born Orthodox Jew who is now an Israeli citizen. For nearly a quarter century, Young has understood the prophesied restoration of both Houses, and has endeavored to awaken Ephraimites to their identity. He has even changed his career field, going through the arduous process of becoming a licensed Israeli tour guide so that he can introduce returning Ephraimites to the Promised Land, and build bridges between Ephraim and Judah.[15]

Young is truly an exception in that he took note of the Torah Awakening even before most Christians became aware of it, and recognized it as the awakening of Ephraim. Another Jewish observer who has taken note of this awakening is Dr. Rivkah Lambert Adler, another American-born Israeli who is a contributing author for *The Times of Israel* and *Breaking Israel News*.[16] Her book, *Ten From the Nations: Torah Awakening Among Non-Jews*, features essays by over 40 contributors from around the world. Many of the contributors are self-identified Ephraimites who have come from traditional Christian backgrounds, while others are Jews who have recognized this growing phenomenon. Adler does not attempt to draw any conclusions in her work, but rather to draw attention to it. In introducing her work, she writes:

> All over the world, current and former Christians are becoming aware of Torah. They are learning about, and implementing, what most of the world thinks of as Jewish practices, including celebrating Shabbat and the Biblical holidays. They are refraining from eating pork and shellfish. They are studying Torah and seeing the Land of Israel, and

---

[15] Hanoch Young, "Meet the Guide," *Kol Yehuda*, accessed September 8, 2017, http://www.kolyehuda.com/Meet-The-Guide.html; Hanoch Young, "For the Time They Are A Changin'," *United2Restore*, December 12, 2016, accessed October 25, 2017, http://www.united2restore.com/2016/12/12/for-the-time-they-are-a-changin/.
[16] "Rivkah Lambert Adler," *The Times of Israel*, accessed October 19, 2017, http://blogs.timesofisrael.com/author/rivkah-lambert-adler/; "About Dr. Rivkah Lambert Adler," *Breaking Israel News*, accessed October 19, 2017, https://www.breakingisraelnews.com/author/rivkahadler/#/.

especially the return of the Jewish people to the Land of Israel, in a new light. They are building positive relationships with the Jewish people.

A huge paradigm shift is happening. With this book, I am like a sociocultural anthropologist, attempting to map the phenomenon of this Torah awakening in all its facets. My hope is that someday soon, what is being introduced in these pages will be common knowledge, as it says in Yeshayahu (Isaiah) 11:9: *The land shall be full of the knowledge of the Lord as water covers the sea bed.*[17]

Perhaps the most significant recent Jewish statement on this subject comes from Rabbi Nachman Kahana, a highly respected Israeli rabbi who has made considerable scholarly contributions to the restoration of the Levitical priesthood and the Temple. In a recent commentary, Rav Kahana wrote:

> The wide expanse of the Golan is waiting for millions of Jews to settle there and infuse the area with Torah life. Yehuda [Judea], Shomron [Samaria], the Negev and Galil [Galilee], will be settled by tens if not hundreds of millions of Jews returning home.
> From where will all these Jews come?
> For this we have to think "outside of the box".
> They will not come from the Jewish community in the United States which is quickly dwindling through intermarriage, coupled with apathy and antagonism of most orthodox Jews towards God's greatest miracle of the last 2000 years. The Jews of Western Europe and South America are following suit.
> The 70 plus years of opportunity for the Jews in the West to return home is rapidly ending, for the timetable of HaShem waits for no man.
> The big numbers will come from the hundreds of millions of Jewish descendants of the Ten Tribes and Anusim (people forced to abandon Judaism and adopt a different religion), who will awaken one day to their Jewish heritage. They are

---

[17] Rivkah Lambert Adler, Ph.D., ed., *Ten from the Nations: Torah Awakening Among Non-Jews* (Jerusalem: Geula Watch Press, 2017), xv-xvi.

the Jewish nation of the future, as prophesied by Yechezkel [Ezekiel] (11:17).[18]

Let us not miss the astounding message in Rav Kahana's bold statement. Although he identifies these returning Israelites as Jews, the fact is that they will be both Jews of the House of Judah and non-Jewish Israelites of the House of Ephraim. All of them are Hebrews who are now or soon will awaken to a Hebraic identity they lost in ages past. This is the understanding Hanoch Young presents in his assessment of Rav Kahana's commentary:

> The thing that is HUGE about what he said is that for many in the Jewish ('Orthodox') community, the feeling is generally, that the Tribes must have already returned. You see, Jewish communities around the world sent emissaries looking for our lost brothers and sisters for centuries. However, once it was determined that there were no longer parts of the world that remained unexplored – where could they be hiding? So, it was assumed that somehow, when no one noticed, they kind of snuck back in among their long-lost Jewish brothers and sisters. Considering the amount of prophecies that speak of an enormous multitude returning to the Land & people of Israel, I could never take that theory/explanation seriously. I mean, how could such a momentous fulfillment of prophecy, the restoration of ALL of Israel, already occurred and no one 'noticed?'

> But, Rav Nachman Kahana is the first prominent Rabbi to publicly come out and say that those lost tribes would come from those totally "distant" from their heritage; does that sound like someone you might know? Does it not fit perfectly with so many non-Jews coming to… or perhaps returning to, the Torah? Rav Nachman even quotes the verse from Yechezkel (Ezekiel) 11:17 – "This is what the Lord says: I will gather you from the nations and bring you back from the countries where you have been scattered, and I will give you back the land of Israel again." Perhaps he is using

---

[18] Rabbi Nachman Kahana, "Ki Taitzai 5777: Gathering the Ten Tribes from faraway lands," RabbiNachmanKahana.com, August 29, 2017, accessed September 8, 2017, http://nachmankahana.com/ki-taitzai-5777/.

words and phrases you might not have chosen, but he is still saying the same things we have been saying. He even quotes from the Malbim (famed Biblical commentator of the 19th Century) who, in explaining the verse above from Yechezkel, wrote: "In the future, HaShem will gather the Ten Tribes from faraway lands, those that did not return at the time of the second Temple, and I will give them the land of Israel."[19]

In this, Rav Kahana affirms what the rabbis have known: that the 48th chapter of Ezekiel promises not only that all the tribes will return, but that each receives a specific allotment of territory, just as in the original conquest of the Promised Land. In order for these verses to be fulfilled, the tribes must be identifiable, something anticipated in the vision recorded by the Apostle John:

> And he carried me away in the Spirit to a great and high mountain, and showed me the holy city, Jerusalem, coming down out of heaven from God, having the glory of God. Her brilliance was like a very costly stone, as a stone of crystal-clear jasper. **It had a great and high wall, with twelve gates**, and at the gates twelve angels; and **names *were* written on them, which are *the names* of the twelve tribes of the sons of Israel**. *There were* three gates on the east and three gates on the north and three gates on the south and three gates on the west. And the wall of the city had twelve foundation stones, and on them *were* the twelve names of the twelve apostles of the Lamb. (Revelation 21:10-14, emphasis added)

Though Christendom tends to view this passage metaphorically, John's vision matches, quite literally, the expectation of the Prophets. The rabbis are right! The ten "Lost Tribes" have not returned, but they will. The great conundrum is what they will look like. I believe the solution to the riddle is exactly answered in the restoration of Two Houses, each of which has played a unique role

---

[19] Hanoch Young, "Who WILL Populate the Land of Israel in the Future?," United 2 Restore, September 18, 2017, accessed September 22, 2017, http://www.united2restore.com/2017/09/18/who-will-populate-the-land-of-israel-in-the-future/.

in the eternal plan of Redemption established from the foundation of the world.

No wonder Paul extolled,

> Oh, the depth of the riches both of the wisdom and knowledge of God! How unsearchable are His judgments and unfathomable His ways! For WHO HAS KNOWN THE MIND OF THE LORD, OR WHO BECAME HIS COUNSELOR? Or WHO HAS FIRST GIVEN TO HIM THAT IT MIGHT BE PAID BACK TO HIM AGAIN? For from Him and through Him and to Him are all things. To Him *be* the glory forever. Amen. (Romans 11:33-36)

## DIVISION OF THE KINGDOM

After the death of Solomon, the tribe of Ephraim led a rebellion that split the nation into the Northern Kingdom of Israel and the Southern Kingdom of Judah. (1 Kings 12).

Hurlbut, *Bible Atlas*, 86.

# 6

# ONE KINGDOM, TWO DESTINIES

**Death and Transfiguration**

As we have seen, even though there is no consistent rabbinic ruling on the question of whether the Lost Tribes will return, there is enough expectation of their return to have fueled Jewish searches for the missing tribes over the centuries. It is still a subject of daily prayers offered by Jews all over the world. The *Shemoneh Esrei* (Eighteen Blessings), also known as the *Amidah* (Standing Prayer), has been the core prayer of Judaism since the return from exile in Babylon. The modern version of the *Amidah* includes this petition:

> Sound the great shofar for our freedom, raise the banner to gather our exiles and gather us together from the four corners of the earth. Blessed are You, HASHEM, Who gathers in the dispersed of His people Israel.[1]

How are these exiles to return? That is the great question.

If there is anything we know about Almighty God, it is that he wants to make sure there is no doubt he has done a thing. That is why he declares the end from the beginning, and why he does the impossible. If the return of the House of Judah has been highly improbable, the return of the House of Israel is impossible. The Jews, at least, have remained a distinct people group regardless of the attempts to annihilate them over the centuries. Their very survival and the establishment of the Jewish State of Israel testify to God's providence. Indeed, he has done many impossible things in the course of reconstituting the Jewish nation and bringing them back to the Promised Land.

The House of Israel, however, is another matter. There is a reason scripture associates the Lost Tribes with the image of a divorced

---

[1] Scherman, Nosson, and Meir Zlotowitz, eds. *The Complete ArtScroll Siddur*. 3rd ed. Brooklyn, New York: Mesorah Publications, Ltd, 2006.

woman, and of a long-lost, presumably dead, son. Scripture also uses the image of a fruitless fig tree to describe the rebellion of and judgment upon the House of Israel – a tree that is, in essence, dead and useless.[2]

Everyone understands the impossibility of bringing the dead back to life, unless, of course, one is YHVH, the Creator of life. What few people understand, though, is the impossibility of a divorced woman being reunited with her estranged husband. The Torah clearly states that a divorced woman cannot remarry her former husband. Let us look again at the relevant passage:

> When a man takes a wife and marries her, and it happens that she finds no favor in his eyes because he has found some indecency in her, and he writes her a certificate of divorce and puts *it* in her hand and sends her out from his house, and she leaves his house and goes and becomes another man's *wife*, and if the latter husband turns against her and writes her a certificate of divorce and puts *it* in her hand and sends her out of his house, or if the latter husband dies who took her to be his wife, **then her former husband who sent her away is not allowed to take her again to be his wife, since she has been defiled; for that is an abomination before the LORD**, and you shall not bring sin on the land which the LORD your God gives you as an inheritance. (Deuteronomy 24:1-4, emphasis added)

This presents a conundrum regarding the return of the House of Israel. Isaiah, Jeremiah, and Hosea testify that YHVH divorced the House of Israel and cut them off from his Covenant. Even though the House of Judah also acted unfaithfully, they remained in the Covenant. This measure of mercy was part of the Father's Kingdom plan, enabling Judah to serve as the visible witness down through the ages that YHVH remains faithful to his Covenant promises to all of Israel.

---

[2] The fruitless fig tree is a picture of both Houses in their state of apostasy. YHVH noted the barrenness of Israel and Judah as both a reason for judgment on them, and, when their enemies destroyed the fruit trees in their land, as a symbol of that judgment. See Jeremiah 5:14-17, 8:13; Hosea 2:12-13, 9:10; Joel 1:12; Habakkuk 3:17-18; Haggai 2:19; Matthew 21:18-22; Luke 13:6-9.

If God is faithful to Judah, then we can trust him to be faithful to Ephraim as well. Which brings us to a passage from Jeremiah that has puzzled the rabbis:

> *God* says, "If a husband divorces his wife and she goes from him and belongs to another man, will he still return to her? Will not that land be completely polluted? But you are a harlot *with* many lovers; yet you turn to Me," declares the LORD. (Jeremiah 3:1)

How can God promise to take Israel back as his bride if he has divorced her and she has given herself to other lovers? If he does so, he breaks his own Law. And if God breaks his own Law, then the whole of the Law is made null and void.

Yet this is precisely the picture he has given the world through Hosea. Whereas Jeremiah wrote about this drama, Hosea lived it out. God directed the prophet to take a prostitute as his wife. Then, when she left him and returned to her life of prostitution, God told Hosea to redeem her out of that life once again and take her home. Had Hosea lived in Judah, perhaps he could not have carried out that action, but he lived in Israel, where adherence to Torah was neither required nor desired. Hence the harlotry of faithless Israel, and the extreme example of Hosea's marriage to a prostitute to illustrate it.

Hosea took Gomer back for the purpose of fulfilling a prophetic picture. Yet as extreme as it is, we do not see Hosea issuing a divorce decree to Gomer as God had done with the harlot Israel. How, then, could God make Hosea's prophetic picture a reality without making the entire Torah of no effect? The Christian answer might be, "There is no problem here; Jesus did away with the Law, so it is no longer applicable to his followers." Yet that does not take into account the words of Jesus/Yeshua Himself:

> Do not think that I came to abolish the Law or the Prophets; I did not come to abolish but to fulfill. For truly I say to you, until heaven and earth pass away, not the smallest letter or stroke shall pass from the Law until all is accomplished. Whoever then annuls one of the least of these commandments, and teaches others *to do* the same, shall be

called least in the kingdom of heaven; but whoever keeps and teaches *them*, he shall be called great in the kingdom of heaven. (Matthew 5:17-19)

But it is easier for heaven and earth to pass away than for one stroke of a letter of the Law to fail. (Luke 16:17)

It would seem that the legal provisions by which the Almighty established our universe are still the principles by which it operates. Therefore it is reasonable to state that if God breaks his own Law, then his ability to govern the universe could be called into question. How, then, can he keep his promise to remarry his divorced spouse? Either he breaks his Law, or he reneges on his promise and is proved faithless, casting doubt on his willingness and ability to fulfill any and all of his promises.

There is only one remedy: someone must die. If death occurs, then all penalties are paid and the offender may start fresh. Specifically, the husband in the marriage covenant must die. If he dies, then the adulterous wife is released from him and from the penalty of her sin against him and may start fresh. That is what the Apostle Paul means when he writes:

Or do you not know, brethren (for I am speaking to those who know the law), that the law has jurisdiction over a person as long as he lives? For the married woman is bound by law to her husband while he is living; but if her husband dies, she is released from the law concerning the husband. So then, if while her husband is living she is joined to another man, she shall be called an adulteress; but if her husband dies, she is free from the law, so that she is not an adulteress though she is joined to another man. (Romans 7:1-3)

But if death is the solution, then we have another problem: death is so *final*! How could God overcome this problem of death? The only way is if the one who died somehow comes back to life.

According to the Apostolic Writings, that is precisely what Yeshua did. Claiming to be Almighty God in human form, Yeshua died, taking the penalty of sin for the whole world on himself, and after three days he returned from the grave. Thus he conquered sin and death and made it possible for God to redeem and remarry his bride (Mark 14:61-62; Luke 22:68-71; 1 Corinthians 15:1-28; Philippians 2:5-11). That is why Paul can say:

> Therefore, my brethren, you also were made to die to the Law through the body of Christ, so that you might be joined to another, to Him who was raised from the dead, in order that we might bear fruit for God. For while we were in the flesh, the sinful passions, which were *aroused* by the Law, were at work in the members of our body to bear fruit for death. But now we have been released from the Law, having died to that by which we were bound, so that we serve in newness of the Spirit and not in oldness of the letter. (Romans 7:4-6)

The church has traditionally interpreted this passage to mean that Christians are no longer subject to Torah. That is *not* what Paul wrote; he wrote that the law which barred us from (re)marriage to God is now satisfied not only by the death and resurrection of Messiah, but also by the fact that those who identify with him are also spiritually dead and resurrected. Do you see the beauty of this? God made it possible for two lovers to reunite: Himself, and his beloved Israel. He did that by his own death, and by the resurrection of his bride who already had died spiritually through her sin.

Now we see why God instituted marriage. It was not just a mechanism for social order and procreation, but a living symbol of his relationship with Israel, the bride through whom he can have a relationship with all the peoples of the earth.

## The Faithless Bride Restored

This is the destiny of Ephraim: to stand as the visible witness of YHVH's eternal mercy, and to be the conduit for his saving grace by which he will redeem all the nations. Judah has a hand in this, of course. As Paul says:

> Then what advantage has the Jew? Or what is the benefit of circumcision? Great in every respect. First of all, that they were entrusted with the oracles of God. (Romans 3:1)

> I am telling the truth in Christ, I am not lying, my conscience testifies with me in the Holy Spirit, that I have great sorrow and unceasing grief in my heart. For I could wish that I myself were accursed, *separated* from Christ for the sake of my brethren, my kinsmen according to the flesh, who are Israelites, to whom belongs the adoption as sons, and the glory and the covenants and the giving of the Law and the *temple* service and the promises, whose are the fathers, and from whom is the Christ according to the flesh, who is over all, God blessed forever. Amen. (Romans 9:1-5)

*From the Jews (Judah) comes the knowledge of YHVH through the scriptures, as well as the testimony of how to serve him, and salvation (to which Yeshua himself testified according to John 4:22). From Ephraim comes the demonstration of the Father's unfailing love in taking extreme efforts to redeem back to himself a people estranged from his Covenant, bringing with them others from the nations who accept the testimony of salvation (redemption) through the Messiah.*

All of this hinges on the Messiah. He is the one who provides hope where there is no hope, as Paul says:

> For by grace you have been saved through faith; and that not of yourselves, *it is* the gift of God; not as a result of works, so that no one may boast. For we are His workmanship, created in Christ Jesus for good works, which God prepared beforehand so that we would walk in them.
>
> Therefore remember that formerly you, the Gentiles in the flesh, who are called "Uncircumcision" by the so-called "Circumcision," *which is* performed in the flesh by human hands—*remember* that you were at that time separate from Christ, excluded from the commonwealth of Israel, and strangers to the covenants of promise, having no hope and without God in the world. But now in Christ Jesus you who formerly were far off have been brought near by the blood of Christ. For He Himself is our peace, who made both *groups into* one and broke down the barrier of the dividing wall, by abolishing in His flesh the enmity, *which is* the Law of commandments *contained* in ordinances, so that in Himself

He might make the two into one new man, *thus* establishing peace, and might reconcile them both in one body to God through the cross, by it having put to death the enmity. AND HE CAME AND PREACHED PEACE TO YOU WHO WERE FAR AWAY, AND PEACE TO THOSE WHO WERE NEAR; for through Him we both have our access in one Spirit to the Father. So then you are no longer strangers and aliens, but you are fellow citizens with the saints, and are of God's household, having been built on the foundation of the apostles and prophets, Christ Jesus Himself being the corner *stone*, in whom the whole building, being fitted together, is growing into a holy temple in the Lord, in whom you also are being built together into a dwelling of God in the Spirit. (Ephesians 2:8-22)

The church has rightly concluded from Ephesians 2 that salvation is by grace alone through faith in Messiah Yeshua. The church has also concluded correctly that in Messiah there is no more division among YHVH's people as he makes "the two into one new man."

What the church has missed, though, is the nationality of this "one new man." The emphasis on Grace over Law has led to the conclusion that the division between Jew and Gentile ends when Jews accept Messiah and, in essence, become Christians. This is the fruit of Replacement Theology, the (often unintended) doctrine that the church has replaced the Jewish people as the primary instrument of God's kingdom plans. The church, in other words, has *become* Israel. But is that really what the apostle means?

No, not at all. Paul seems to understand that there are two elements of Israel involved in this process. If I may be so bold, Paul appears to be proclaiming a Two House message. This becomes more clear as we pull the threads of the references Paul uses to build his case, not only to the Ephesians, but in all of his letters.

It should be obvious that Paul and the other New Testament writers quoted extensively from the Tanakh. Notice Paul's admonition to Timothy:

All Scripture is inspired by God and profitable for teaching, for reproof, for correction, for training in righteousness; so that the man of God may be adequate, equipped for every good work. (II Timothy 3:16-17)

When the apostle writes "all scripture," he means everything from Genesis to Malachi. In other words, Moses and the Prophets. That was "all scripture" in the first century; there was no New Testament at that time. As we see in Acts 17:1-3 and 28:23, Paul was in the habit of using these very scriptures to give evidence that Yeshua is the Messiah. In this he followed the precedent established by Yeshua himself (Luke 24:27; John 5:45-46).

What references did Paul use in Ephesians 2? The ones that interest us come from this phrase: "And He came and preached peace to you who were far away, and peace to those who were near." The direct reference is Isaiah 57:19, in a passage prophesying the restoration of Israel's exiles. After restating the idolatrous iniquities of God's Covenant people, the prophet gives these words of comfort:

> And it will be said, "Build up, build up, prepare the way, remove *every* obstacle out of the way of My people."
> For thus says the high and exalted One Who lives forever, whose name is Holy, "I dwell *on* a high and holy place, and *also* with the contrite and lowly of spirit in order to revive the spirit of the lowly and to revive the heart of the contrite. For I will not contend forever, nor will I always be angry; for the spirit would grow faint before Me, and the breath *of those whom* I have made. Because of the iniquity of his unjust gain I was angry and struck him; I hid *My face* and was angry, and he went on turning away, in the way of his heart. I have seen his ways, but I will heal him; I will lead him and restore comfort to him and to his mourners, creating the praise of the lips. **Peace, peace to him who is far and to him who is near," says the LORD, "and I will heal him."** But the wicked are like the tossing sea, for it cannot be quiet, and its waters toss up refuse and mud. "There is no peace," says my God, "for the wicked." (Isaiah 57:14-21, emphasis added)

"He" in this passage is all of Israel. We know this because Isaiah 57 is part of a lengthy series of prophecies regarding the redemption of all Israel, as well as any and all Gentiles ("foreigners") who are willing to join with them. The prophet summarizes these passages in the preceding chapter:

> The Lord GOD, who gathers the dispersed of Israel, declares, "Yet *others* I will gather to them, to those *already* gathered." (Isaiah 56:8)

Paul, the Hebrew of Hebrews, product of the best biblical training available to a Pharisee in the first century (Acts 26:4-6; Philippians 3:2-6), surely knew these passages from Isaiah. In fact, his Ephesian audience knew them, having had the benefit of Paul teaching them for over two years (Acts 19:1-10). Thus, when Paul makes reference to those who are "far" and those who are "near," his Ephesian readers understand him to mean the House of Israel who were removed from the Covenant and scattered to the ends of the earth, and the House of Judah who remained in the Covenant.

## The Dry Tree Revived

But how can we be sure? This is at best a cryptic reference, so if there is any substance to it we should be able to find additional evidence somewhere in the Tanakh. And, indeed we do. It comes from the contrite prayer of repentance uttered by the prophet Daniel on behalf of his people toward the end of the Babylonian Captivity:

> Righteousness belongs to You, O Lord, but to us open shame, as it is this day—to the men of Judah, the inhabitants of Jerusalem and all Israel, **those who are nearby and those who are far away in all the countries to which You have driven them**, because of their unfaithful deeds which they have committed against You. (Daniel 9:7, emphasis added)

There is no question that Daniel knew the signs of his own times. Earlier in the chapter (Daniel 9:1-3), he explained that he began to pray because he understood from the writings of Jeremiah that the 70 years of Judah's exile was nearing an end. Specifically, he referred to this passage from Jeremiah – one verse of which Christians often reference without considering its context:

For thus says the LORD, "When seventy years have been completed for Babylon, I will visit you and fulfill My good word to you, to bring you back to this place. **For I know the plans that I have for you," declares the LORD, "plans for welfare and not for calamity to give you a future and a hope.** Then you will call upon Me and come and pray to Me, and I will listen to you. You will seek Me and find *Me* when you search for Me with all your heart. I will be found by you," declares the LORD, "and I will restore your fortunes and will gather you from all the nations and from all the places where I have driven you," declares the LORD, "and I will bring you back to the place from where I sent you into exile." (Jeremiah 29:10-14, emphasis added)

Is this a promise given only to Judah, or to all Israel? The seventy years portion was to Judah, but the principle is for all Israel. Jeremiah makes that point twice, in passages that Daniel surely understood just as clearly:

"Therefore behold, days are coming," declares the LORD, "when it will no longer be said, 'As the LORD lives, who brought up the sons of Israel out of the land of Egypt,' but, 'As the LORD lives, who brought up the sons of Israel from the land of the north and from all the countries where He had banished them.' For I will restore them to their own land which I gave to their fathers." (Jeremiah 16:14-15, 23:7-8)

And surely Daniel understood what Isaiah said on the subject:

Then it will happen on that day that the Lord will again recover the second time with His hand the remnant of His people, who will remain, from Assyria, Egypt, Pathros, Cush, Elam, Shinar, Hamath, and from the islands of the sea. And He will lift up a standard for the nations and assemble the banished ones of Israel, and will gather the dispersed of Judah from the four corners of the earth. Then the jealousy of Ephraim will depart, and those who harass Judah will be cut off; Ephraim will not be jealous of Judah, and Judah will not harass Ephraim. They will swoop down on the slopes of the Philistines on the west; together they will plunder the sons of the east; they will possess Edom and Moab, and the sons of Ammon will be subject to them. (Isaiah 11:11-14)

Thus, when Daniel set out to intercede on behalf of his people, he was careful to include every component of the Hebrew nation: Judah, Jerusalem, and all Israel. These three references encompass the two Houses and the Holy City, where the Presence of the Almighty rested. That alone should be enough to identify the ones for whom he makes intercession, but then he mentions those "nearby" and those "far away." Who could he mean?

Think for a moment about Daniel's situation. Those nearby are his kin, the Jewish people whom the Babylonians carried away to the place we know as Iraq. Although many Jews fled to Egypt and other places, the primary dwelling of a Jew in Daniel's day would have been either in Babylon or among the remnant in the Holy Land. Most were not scattered as were their fellow Hebrews of the Northern Kingdom. At the time Daniel made his prayer, the House of Israel had been in exile for nearly two centuries, and indeed had been scattered "far away."

Daniel is therefore praying for YHVH to be merciful and forgive the entire nation of Israel, not just the Jewish part. He has authority to do so, for he is a member of the royal household of David.

Moreover, Daniel is a eunuch. This may come as a surprise to many readers, but it is the testimony of scripture. When we first meet Daniel, we learn this about his circumstances:

> In the third year of the reign of Jehoiakim king of Judah, Nebuchadnezzar king of Babylon came to Jerusalem and besieged it. And the Lord gave Jehoiakim king of Judah into his hand, with some of the vessels of the house of God. And he brought them to the land of Shinar, to the house of his god, and placed the vessels in the treasury of his god. **Then the king commanded Ashpenaz, his chief eunuch, to bring some of the people of Israel, both of the royal family and of the nobility, youths without blemish, of good appearance and skillful in all wisdom, endowed with knowledge, understanding learning, and competent to stand in the king's palace**, and to teach them the

literature and language of the Chaldeans. The king assigned them a daily portion of the food that the king ate, and of the wine that he drank. They were to be educated for three years, and at the end of that time they were to stand before the king. Among these were Daniel, Hananiah, Mishael, and Azariah of the tribe of Judah. **And the chief of the eunuchs gave them names: Daniel he called Belteshazzar,** Hananiah he called Shadrach, Mishael he called Meshach, and Azariah he called Abednego. (Daniel 1:1-7 ESV, emphasis added)

Josephus, the great Jewish historian of the first century, attests that Daniel was indeed of the royal household of Judah, and made a eunuch by order of the King of Babylon.[3] Perhaps we should not be surprised to learn that this was another fulfillment of prophecy, this time given to King Hezekiah of Judah regarding the judgment coming on his nation:

Then Isaiah said to Hezekiah, "Hear the word of the LORD of hosts: Behold, the days are coming, when all that is in your house, and that which your fathers have stored up till this day, shall be carried to Babylon. Nothing shall be left, says the LORD. **And some of your own sons, who will come from you, whom you will father, shall be taken away, and they shall be eunuchs in the palace of the king of Babylon.**" Then Hezekiah said to Isaiah, "The word of the LORD that you have spoken is good." For he thought, "There will be peace and security in my days." (Isaiah 39:5-8 ESV, emphasis added)

This is an important point. According to Torah (Deuteronomy 23:1), a eunuch is cut off from the assembly of the Lord. Eunuchs cannot produce seed, or offspring, and therefore they cannot establish a house, or family, of their own. Being unfruitful, they cannot fulfill the first and most basic command YHVH gave to humanity:

---

[3] Flavius Josephus, *The Antiquities of the Jews*, trans. William Whiston (Project Gutenberg, 2009), Book X, Ch. 10, accessed October 25, 2017, http://www.gutenberg.org/files/2848/2848-h/2848-h.htm#link102HCH0010)

> God blessed them; and God said to them, "Be fruitful and multiply, and fill the earth, and subdue it; and rule over the fish of the sea and over the birds of the sky and over every living thing that moves on the earth." (Genesis 1:28)

Such was Daniel's unhappy state. Just as the House of Israel had been cut off for the rebellion which resulted in their unfruitfulness for the Kingdom of YHVH, Daniel also had been cut off because of the physical condition imposed on him which had made him unfruitful. His situation was hopeless, and he could not expect to have a place in the Covenant Nation – except for this promise in that same comforting section of Isaiah:

> Let not the foreigner who has joined himself to the LORD say, "The LORD will surely separate me from His people." Nor let the eunuch say, "Behold, I am a dry tree."
> For thus says the LORD, "To the eunuchs who keep My sabbaths, and choose what pleases Me, and hold fast My covenant, to them I will give in My house and within My walls a memorial, and a name better than that of sons and daughters; I will give them an everlasting name which will not be cut off.
> "Also the foreigners who join themselves to the LORD, to minister to Him, and to love the name of the LORD, to be His servants, every one who keeps from profaning the sabbath and holds fast My covenant; even those I will bring to My holy mountain and make them joyful in My house of prayer. Their burnt offerings and their sacrifices will be acceptable on My altar; for My house will be called a house of prayer for all the peoples." (Isaiah 56:3-7)

## The Barren One Brings Forth Fruit

Paul would surely have known not only Isaiah's prophecy, but Daniel's prayer, and likely also the comfort Daniel derived from Isaiah's words. Daniel had been made a eunuch by men, but Paul had made himself a eunuch for the sake of the kingdom of heaven, in the sense that he refused marriage so that he could pursue the calling the Almighty had placed on him. As he said:

> Yet I wish that all men were even as I myself am. However, each man has his own gift from God, one in this manner, and another in that. But I say to the unmarried and to widows that it is good for them if they remain even as I... But I want you to be free from concern. One who is unmarried is concerned about the things of the Lord, how he may please the Lord... . (1 Corinthians 7:7-8, 32)

Physically speaking, Paul was unfruitful; no physical heir came from his body as far as we know. Yet who can equal the spiritual fruit he produced, and is still producing, for the Kingdom?

Perhaps in this we can understand yet another cryptic reference, this time uttered by Yeshua in the context of a question about – should we be surprised? – marriage and divorce:

> *Some* Pharisees came to Jesus, testing Him and asking, "Is it lawful *for a man* to divorce his wife for any reason at all?" And He answered and said, "Have you not read that He who created *them* from the beginning MADE THEM MALE AND FEMALE, and said, 'FOR THIS REASON A MAN SHALL LEAVE HIS FATHER AND MOTHER AND BE JOINED TO HIS WIFE, AND THE TWO SHALL BECOME ONE FLESH'? So they are no longer two, but one flesh. What therefore God has joined together, let no man separate." They said to Him, "Why then did Moses command to GIVE HER A CERTIFICATE OF DIVORCE AND SEND *her* AWAY?" He said to them, "Because of your hardness of heart Moses permitted you to divorce your wives; but from the beginning it has not been this way. And I say to you, whoever divorces his wife, except for immorality, and marries another woman commits adultery."
> The disciples said to Him, "If the relationship of the man with his wife is like this, it is better not to marry." But He said to them, "Not all men *can* accept this statement, but *only* those to whom it has been given. **For there are eunuchs who were born that way from their mother's womb; and there are eunuchs who were made eunuchs by men; and there are *also* eunuchs who made themselves eunuchs for the sake of the kingdom of heaven.** He who is able to

accept *this*, let him accept *it*." (Matthew 19:3-12, emphasis added)

Ah yes, Yeshua was a eunuch as well, born that way from His mother's womb, if we can accept it. Not a physical eunuch, of course; like Paul, Yeshua was perfectly healthy. He had to be without spot or blemish to fulfill the role of the perfect Lamb of God Who takes away the sin of the world (John 1:29, 36). Unlike Paul, who chose not to marry and have children, Yeshua was destined to have no physical offspring. Thus he was a eunuch from his mother's womb, born to be cut off for the sake of his people. And yet, as Isaiah again tells us, by doing the impossible, the impossible would be done for Yeshua, and he, too, would produce much fruit:

> Behold, My servant will prosper, He will be high and lifted up and greatly exalted. Just as many were astonished at you, *My people*, so His appearance was marred more than any man and His form more than the sons of men. Thus He will sprinkle many nations, Kings will shut their mouths on account of Him; for what had not been told them they will see, and what they had not heard they will understand.
> Who has believed our message? And to whom has the arm of the LORD been revealed? For He grew up before Him like a tender shoot, and like a root out of parched ground; He has no *stately* form or majesty that we should look upon Him, nor appearance that we should be attracted to Him. He was despised and forsaken of men, a man of sorrows and acquainted with grief; and like one from whom men hide their face He was despised, and we did not esteem Him.
> Surely our griefs He Himself bore, and our sorrows He carried; yet we ourselves esteemed Him stricken, smitten of God, and afflicted. But He was pierced through for our transgressions, He was crushed for our iniquities; the chastening for our well-being *fell* upon Him, and by His scourging we are healed. All of us like sheep have gone astray, each of us has turned to his own way; but the LORD has caused the iniquity of us all to fall on Him.
> He was oppressed and He was afflicted, yet He did not open His mouth; like a lamb that is led to slaughter, and like a

sheep that is silent before its shearers, so He did not open His mouth. By oppression and judgment He was taken away; and as for His generation, who considered that He was cut off out of the land of the living for the transgression of my people, to whom the stroke *was due*? His grave was assigned with wicked men, yet He was with a rich man in His death, because He had done no violence, nor was there any deceit in His mouth.
But the LORD was pleased to crush Him, putting *Him* to grief; if He would render Himself *as* a guilt offering, He will see *His* offspring, He will prolong *His* days, and the good pleasure of the LORD will prosper in His hand. As a result of the anguish of His soul, He will see *it and* be satisfied; by His knowledge the Righteous One, My Servant, will justify the many, as He will bear their iniquities. Therefore, I will allot Him a portion with the great, and He will divide the booty with the strong; because He poured out Himself to death, and was numbered with the transgressors; yet He Himself bore the sin of many, and interceded for the transgressors. (Isaiah 52:13 – 53:12)

These three – Yeshua, Paul, and Daniel – proclaimed the merciful grace of God in reconciling to Himself not only the Houses of Judah and Israel, but through them the Gentiles of every nation. Everyone, whether far off or near. Paul the Apostle understood this, and so did his colleague Peter. After that great sermon on the day of Pentecost (Shavuot), when the Holy Spirit empowered Yeshua's followers to speak the Gospel of the Kingdom with boldness, Peter gave this answer to those who asked what they should do with this news:

> Repent, and each of you be baptized in the name of Jesus Christ for the forgiveness of your sins; and you will receive the gift of the Holy Spirit. **For the promise is for you and your children and for all who are far off**, as many as the Lord our God will call to Himself. (Acts 2:38-39, emphasis added)

If Peter and Paul understood the Messianic mission of reconciling the two Houses, who else among the Apostles understood it?

# Two Angry Brothers, Part 1:
# LEVI

Jacob's final words to his sons include this less-than-pleasant pronouncement on two of them:

> Simeon and Levi are brothers; their swords are implements of violence. Let my soul not enter into their council; let not my glory be united with their assembly; because in their anger they slew men, and in their self-will they lamed oxen. Cursed be their anger, for it is fierce; and their wrath, for it is cruel. I will disperse them in Jacob, and scatter them in Israel. (Genesis 49:5-7)

A defining characteristic of Simeon and Levi is anger – such as that which drove them to massacre the men of Shechem to avenge the honor of their sister Dinah (Genesis 34). That incident is what prompted their father to "bless" them with dispersion throughout Israel.

Levi did not receive a territorial allotment in the Promised Land because God chose them as the priestly tribe to minister in the Temple. Oddly enough, Levi's anger brought this about: when Israel sinned by making and worshipping a golden calf, the Levites rallied to Moses and killed 3,000 of the rebels (Exodus 32:25-29, Numbers 3:5-13, 25:7-13, Deuteronomy 18:1).

Forty years later, Israel again engaged in idolatry at Baal-Peor - this time involving sexual liaisons with foreign women in the worship of their gods. Moved by righteous anger, Phinehas (Pinchas), grandson of Aaron the High Priest, took a spear and killed both the Israelite ringleader of the rebellion and the Moabite woman he had brought into the camp. This moved the Lord to place on Phinehas the covenant of peace, something which He promises eventually to place on all Israel when the tribes are restored (Numbers 25:7-13, Isaiah 54:9-10, Ezekiel 34:25, 37:15-28).

The lesson for us? That Levi's descendants found a way to humble themselves before the Almighty and channel their anger into zeal for His House.

Levi's priestly role is depicted in this Israeli postage stamp, one of a series that honors the twelve tribes. The symbol is the breastplate of the high priest, along with a quote from Deuteronomy 33:10, "They shall teach Your ordinances to Jacob, and Your law to Israel." G. Hamori, designer, "Stamp of Israel–Tribes–30mil–Levi. Second definitive series," (State of Israel, November 8, 1955).
Public domain, via Wikimedia Commons, https://commons.wikimedia.org/wiki/File%3AStamp_of_Israel_-Tribes - 30mil.jpg.

# 7

# APOSTOLIC EXPECTATIONS, PART 1: A MESSAGE FOR TWO BROTHERS

### The New Testament's Foundation in the Old Testament

The four gospel writers took great pains to point out the elements of Yeshua's life that fulfilled messianic prophecies of the Tanakh. Taken at face value, they provide an impressive number of specific data points demonstrating the intersection of the Divine Plan of redemption in the life of the Messiah.

They begin with the accounts of Yeshua's birth and early childhood. Any good Christian teacher should be able to explain how God orchestrated events for Mary and Joseph to ensure that this Galilean couple became parents of an immaculately conceived child (Isaiah 7:14) in Bethlehem, the hometown of King David (Micah 5:2). What they likely cannot explain, however, is why these prophecies appear in passages related to the exile and return of both Houses of Israel. That requires deeper study; probing under the surface to find out why the Apostles chose those specific verses from those specific passages to make their case.

Consider the example of this reference in Matthew's account:

> Now when they [the Magi] had gone, behold, an angel of the Lord appeared to Joseph in a dream and said, "Get up! Take the Child and His mother and flee to Egypt, and remain there until I tell you; for Herod is going to search for the Child to destroy Him." So Joseph got up and took the Child and His mother while it was still night, and left for Egypt. He remained there until the death of Herod. *This was* to fulfill what had been spoken by the Lord through the prophet: **"OUT OF EGYPT I CALLED MY SON."** (Matthew 2:13-15, emphasis added)

The surface reading tells us that God established another "divine coincidence" to make sure his Messiah would repeat the Exodus of Israel from Egypt. But why? Maybe if we look at the reference itself we can find the answer. It comes from Hosea 11:

> When Israel *was* a youth I loved him, and **out of Egypt I called My son.** The more they called them, the more they went from them; they kept sacrificing to the Baals and burning incense to idols. **Yet it is I who taught Ephraim to walk, I took them in My arms; but they did not know that I healed them.** I led them with cords of a man, with bonds of love, and I became to them as one who lifts the yoke from their jaws; and I bent down *and* fed them.
> They will not return to the land of Egypt; but Assyria—he will be their king because they refused to return *to Me*. The sword will whirl against their cities, and will demolish their gate bars and consume *them* because of their counsels. So My people are bent on turning from Me. Though they call them to *the One* on high, none at all exalts *Him*.
> **How can I give you up, O Ephraim? How can I surrender you, O Israel?** How can I make you like Admah? How can I treat you like Zeboiim? My heart is turned over within Me, all My compassions are kindled. **I will not execute My fierce anger; I will not destroy Ephraim again.** For I am God and not man, the Holy One in your midst, and I will not come in wrath. They will walk after the LORD, He will roar like a lion; indeed He will roar and *His* sons will come trembling from the west. They will come trembling like birds from Egypt and like doves from the land of Assyria; and I will settle them in their houses, declares the LORD.
> **Ephraim surrounds Me with lies and the house of Israel with deceit; Judah is also unruly against God**, even against the Holy One who is faithful. (Hosea 11:1-12, emphasis added)

How curious. Matthew's reference to Yeshua spending his childhood in Egypt appears in a prophetic text about YHVH's unending love for Ephraim and promise to restore this part of the nation of Israel. This is the Holy One's declaration regardless of the fact that Ephraim continues in blatant rebellion against him. Of course, Judah is not blameless; the word to Hosea is clear on that. Even so, this particular prophecy clearly has special emphasis on the House of Ephraim. They, not Judah, were exiled to Assyria, but they, like Judah, will return again – trembling in fear and repentance from the west and everywhere else the Lord has scattered them. This is consistent with God's promise not to "destroy Ephraim again," and not to make them like Admah and Zeboiim, allies of Sodom and Gomorrah which were destroyed when God judged those cities (Genesis 14, 19; Deuteronomy 29:23).

This testimony of God's love for Ephraim even when he is in rebellion brings to mind something another apostle wrote:

> For while we were still helpless, at the right time Christ died for the ungodly. **For one will hardly die for a righteous man; though perhaps for the good man someone would dare even to die. But God demonstrates His own love toward us, in that while we were yet sinners, Christ died for us.** Much more then, having now been justified by His blood, we shall be saved from the wrath *of God* through Him. For if while we were enemies we were reconciled to God through the death of His Son, much more, having been reconciled, we shall be saved by His life. And not only this, but we also exult in God through our Lord Jesus Christ, through whom we have now received the reconciliation. (Romans 5:6-11, emphasis added)

Could it be that Paul's inference here in Romans specifically concerns the restoration of Ephraim? The consistent Christian position on this passage in Romans 5 and similar passages is that God's love for the entire world motivated him to redeem it at the cost of his own beloved son even though the world was in rebellion against him. That is the message from what is possibly the most familiar verse in all the Apostolic Writings:

> For God so loved the world, that He gave His only begotten Son, that whoever believes in Him shall not perish, but have eternal life. (John 3:16)

This Christian perspective is not incorrect; God does indeed love the entire world, and he has labored to redeem it since our first ancestors rebelled against him in the Garden of Eden. However, the Scripture is clear that God's vehicle of redemption is the Covenant Nation of Israel. The Almighty did not reveal himself to any other people, and did not choose any other people for himself. That is why Paul in particular writes about Gentiles becoming part of the commonwealth of Israel (Ephesians 2), being grafted into the olive tree of Israel (Romans 11), and being of the one and only seed of Abraham (Galatians 3).

As we shall see in our investigation of the New Covenant, YHVH did not extend salvation to any other nation than Israel. More specifically, when he declared the New Covenant, he stated that he would make it with the House of Israel and the House of Judah (Jeremiah 31:31-34; Hebrews 8:8-12). Therefore, whoever will avail themselves of this salvation must somehow become affiliated with the nation of Israel.

## The Harmony of Salvation and Redemption

There is a nuance here that escapes the casual Christian. The church emphasizes *salvation*, meaning a supernatural rescue from destruction in the wrathful judgment of an angry God. That is indeed correct. However, the church also teaches about being redeemed by the blood of the Lamb (1 Peter 1:17-20). Something that is redeemed must at one time have been owned by the redeemer. What, in this context, would that be? Although God does indeed own the earth and everything in it (Psalm 24:1, 89:11; 1 Corinthians 10:26), the only nation he claims as a special possession is Israel (Exodus 19:5-6; Deuteronomy 4:20, 7:6, 14:2, 26:18; Psalm 135:4; Titus 2:11-14; 1 Peter 2:9). In fact, it is not until the end of the Bible that we read this heavenly declaration:

> Then the seventh angel sounded; and there were loud voices in heaven, saying, "The kingdom of the world has become *the kingdom* of our Lord and of His Christ; and He will reign forever and ever." (Revelation 11:15)

How, then, can God redeem what was not his? Nations, of course, were his idea; he created them through his judgment on mankind during the Tower of Babel incident (Genesis 11:1-9). Having just destroyed a united and rebellious humanity in the Great Flood, he was not about to repeat that judgment until his plan of redemption could be set in motion.

That plan involved a man named Abraham, through whom YHVH would establish a chosen seed (Genesis 12:1-3). That word "seed" should remind us of a parable Yeshua spoke:

> He presented another parable to them, saying, "The kingdom of heaven is like a mustard seed, which a man took and sowed in his field; and this is smaller than all *other* seeds, but when it is full grown, it is larger than the garden plants and becomes a tree, so that THE BIRDS OF THE AIR come and NEST IN ITS BRANCHES." (Matthew 13:31-32)

The chosen seed God established in Abraham became the nation of Israel. That nation, in turn, became the Kingdom of Israel, a kingdom destined to be synonymous with the Kingdom of Heaven or the Kingdom of God. We know this because there is only one nation God has promised to preserve forever, and that is Israel. Moreover, God has stated that his Kingdom will overcome and rule all other kingdoms, even to the point that there will be no recognizable trace of those earthly kingdoms. The prophecies of Jeremiah and Daniel present this from two perspectives:

> Thus says the LORD, Who gives the sun for light by day and the fixed order of the moon and the stars for light by night, Who stirs up the sea so that its waves roar; the LORD of hosts is His name: **"If this fixed order departs from before Me," declares the LORD, "Then the offspring of Israel also will cease from being a nation before Me forever."** (Jeremiah 31:35-36)

> "But as for you, O Jacob My servant, do not fear, nor be dismayed, O Israel! For, see, I am going to save you from afar, and your descendants from the land of their captivity; and Jacob will return and be undisturbed and secure, with no one making him tremble. O Jacob My servant, do not fear,"

declares the Lord, "For I am with you. **For I will make a full end of all the nations where I have driven you, yet I will not make a full end of you**; but I will correct you properly and by no means leave you unpunished." (Jeremiah 46:27-28, emphasis added)

**In the days of those kings the God of heaven will set up a kingdom which will never be destroyed, and *that* kingdom will not be left for another people; it will crush and put an end to all these kingdoms, but it will itself endure forever.** Inasmuch as you saw that a stone was cut out of the mountain without hands and that it crushed the iron, the bronze, the clay, the silver and the gold, the great God has made known to the king what will take place in the future; so the dream is true and its interpretation is trustworthy." (Daniel 2:44-45, emphasis added)

Jeremiah delivered his prophecies as an old man at roughly the same time Daniel as a young man delivered the word of the Lord to King Nebuchadnezzar of Babylon. Both prophets witnessed the Babylonian conquest of Judah. Since the Northern Kingdom of Israel had fallen to Assyria nearly a century before Jeremiah's birth, the destruction of Judah plunged both prophets into despair for the Covenant promises of the Almighty. Thus the need for God to give each man reassurance, and through them to remind both Houses of Israel as well as their captors that the Lord was not slack in keeping his promises. He had not cast aside either House, but had a plan to redeem each and ensure they fulfilled their prophetic destinies.

### Parables of the Kingdom in Context

The central feature of those prophetic destinies is that the Two Houses exist to call all people into relationship with the Living God. In a corporate sense, that means somehow becoming part of this holy Kingdom – a message Yeshua proclaimed in parables of the Kingdom such as these:

> The kingdom of heaven is like a treasure hidden in the field, which a man found and hid *again*; and from joy over it he goes and sells all that he has and buys that field.
> Again, the kingdom of heaven is like a merchant seeking fine pearls, and upon finding one pearl of great value, he went and sold all that he had and bought it.
> Again, the kingdom of heaven is like a dragnet cast into the sea, and gathering *fish* of every kind; and when it was filled, they drew it up on the beach; and they sat down and gathered the good *fish* into containers, but the bad they threw away. So it will be at the end of the age; the angels will come forth and take out the wicked from among the righteous, and will throw them into the furnace of fire; in that place there will be weeping and gnashing of teeth. (Matthew 13:44-50)

Yeshua, of course, was not the first to proclaim this Gospel of the Kingdom. One could make the case that Moses had that particular honor. Centuries after the Almighty called Abraham to this covenant purpose, Moses explained this to Abraham's descendants:

> **The LORD did not set His love on you nor choose you because you were more in number than any of the peoples, for you were the fewest of all peoples, but because the LORD loved you and kept the oath which He swore to your forefathers, the LORD brought you out by a mighty hand and redeemed you from the house of slavery**, from the hand of Pharaoh king of Egypt. Know therefore that the LORD your God, He is God, the faithful God, who keeps His covenant and His lovingkindness to a thousandth generation with those who love Him and keep His commandments; but repays those who hate Him to their faces, to destroy them; He will not delay with him who hates Him, He will repay him to his face. Therefore, you shall keep the commandment and the statutes and the judgments which I am commanding you today, to do them. (Deuteronomy 7:7-11, emphasis added)

Another apostle, John, echoed these words of Moses:

> In this is love, not that we loved God, but that He loved us and sent His Son *to be* the propitiation for our sins. (1 John 4:10)

"Propitiation" is a big word. It means atonement; the payment for a debt. In this case, the debt of sin. If we have any doubt about the definition of sin, John spells it out for us in the same place where he explains the remedy for it:

> Everyone who practices sin also practices lawlessness; and sin is lawlessness. You know that He appeared in order to take away sins; and in Him there is no sin. (1 John 3:4-5)

If the Torah is God's Law, then what John means here is that *lawlessness* is *Torahlessness*. In other words, sin is disregard of God's Torah – his Law, Teaching, Commandments. Yeshua, therefore, came to pay the debt for Torahlessness and make it possible to enter once again into fellowship with the Creator. His atoning death on the execution stake (the cross) is the same as the atonement the High Priest made for the nation of Israel each year on Yom Kippur, the Day of Atonement (Exodus 30:1-10; Leviticus 16:1-34; John 1:29-36; Hebrews 7:26-28, 9:11-28).

The question, then, is how one can be redeemed to be included once more into a covenant of which he or she has never been a member. The Covenant YHVH established was with Abraham and Abraham's seed, meaning Israel. Speaking once again through Moses, he made this abundantly clear on the day he renewed that Covenant with the nation at Sinai:

> Moses went up to God, and the LORD called to him from the mountain, saying, "Thus you shall say to the house of Jacob and tell the sons of Israel: 'You yourselves have seen what I did to the Egyptians, and *how* I bore you on eagles' wings, and brought you to Myself. **Now then, if you will indeed obey My voice and keep My covenant, then you shall be My own possession among all the peoples, for all the earth is Mine; and you shall be to Me a kingdom of priests and a holy nation.'** These are the words that you shall speak to the sons of Israel."

> So Moses came and called the elders of the people, and set before them all these words which the LORD had commanded him. **All the people answered together and said, "All that the LORD has spoken we will do!"** And Moses brought back the words of the people to the LORD. (Exodus 19:3-8, emphasis added)

If we accept this testimony of Scripture, then Israel is indeed unique among all the nations of the earth. Only Israel has received the Torah of the Living God, and only Israel has been claimed by him as his special possession. All he required of this seed of Abraham was to obey his voice and keep his Covenant. God did not explain why at that point, but Moses did forty years later. The explanation came when the next generation had completed the testing in the wilderness and were ready to embark on their life mission of possessing the Promised Land while simultaneously serving as instruments of God's judgment on the wicked nations dwelling there:

> See, I have taught you statutes and judgments just as the LORD my God commanded me, that you should do thus in the land where you are entering to possess it. **So keep and do *them*, for that is your wisdom and your understanding in the sight of the peoples who will hear all these statutes and say, "Surely this great nation is a wise and understanding people."** For what great nation is there that has a god so near to it as is the LORD our God whenever we call on Him? Or what great nation is there that has statutes and judgments as righteous as this whole law which I am setting before you today? (Deuteronomy 4:5-8, emphasis added)

The implied meaning of Moses' words is that all the peoples of the earth would see Israel living in true peace, security, and blessing, and would make the connection that this happy state was a direct result of their obedience to the Lord God. The stories of such foreigners as Rahab and Ruth (Joshua 2:1-21, 6:22-25; Ruth 1:15-22) demonstrate how this happened in ancient days. As we have seen, Isaiah also testifies to Israel's national redemptive purpose:

> Also the foreigners who join themselves to the LORD, to minister to Him, and to love the name of the LORD, to be His servants, every one who keeps from profaning the sabbath and holds fast My covenant; even those I will bring to My holy mountain and make them joyful in My house of prayer. Their burnt offerings and their sacrifices will be acceptable on My altar; for My house will be called a house of prayer for all the peoples. (Isaiah 56:7-8; see also Matthew 21:12-13; Mark 11:15-17; Luke 19:45-48)

Thus Israel would be a living example, able to make disciples from other nations simply through the process of walking out the commandments of YHVH and teaching others as opportunity arose.

Christian ears should hear something familiar in this national mission. It is, after all, exactly what Messiah Yeshua commanded his followers:

> And Jesus came up and spoke to them, saying, "All authority has been given to Me in heaven and on earth. **Go therefore and make disciples of all the nations, baptizing them in the name of the Father and the Son and the Holy Spirit, teaching them to observe all that I commanded you**; and lo, I am with you always, even to the end of the age." (Matthew 28:18-20, emphasis added)

This may come as a surprise to many, but the testimony of Scripture is clear: the "Great Commission" of the Christian church is the same commission YHVH gave to the nation of Israel. By now the reason should be clear: the church is not a new creation, but a central part of the restoration of the House of Israel. Even as the Jewish people have been fulfilling Judah's commission for centuries simply by holding fast to Torah and living as best they can by its standards, the other part of Israel, the hidden part, has been calling the people of the earth to Torah without knowing exactly what they were doing.

## Calling the World to Torah, Christian Style

What? Christians keeping Torah? It sounds strange, but when we consider it, those who have taken the commandments of Yeshua seriously have done exactly that. Although the church has discarded the Sabbath and the Feasts of the Lord, among other important aspects of Torah, and has included in the worship of God a mixture of elements not specified in his Word, the fact remains that the highest priority of a true Christian is to love God and love other people. When Yeshua identified the greatest commandments, he quoted directly from the Torah:

> One of the scribes came and heard them arguing, and recognizing that He had answered them well, asked Him, "What commandment is the foremost of all?" Jesus answered, **"The foremost is, 'HEAR, O ISRAEL! THE LORD OUR GOD IS ONE LORD; AND YOU SHALL LOVE THE LORD YOUR GOD WITH ALL YOUR HEART, AND WITH ALL YOUR SOUL, AND WITH ALL YOUR MIND, AND WITH ALL YOUR STRENGTH.' The second is this, 'YOU SHALL LOVE YOUR NEIGHBOR AS YOURSELF.'** There is no other commandment greater than these." The scribe said to Him, "Right, Teacher; You have truly stated that HE IS ONE, AND THERE IS NO ONE ELSE BESIDES HIM; AND TO LOVE HIM WITH ALL THE HEART AND WITH ALL THE UNDERSTANDING AND WITH ALL THE STRENGTH, AND TO LOVE ONE'S NEIGHBOR AS HIMSELF, is much more than all burnt offerings and sacrifices." When Jesus saw that he had answered intelligently, He said to him, "You are not far from the kingdom of God." (Mark 12:28-34, emphasis added. See also Deuteronomy 6:4-9, Leviticus 19:18; 1 Samuel 15:22; Hosea 6:6; Micah 6:6-8.)

Why would Yeshua quote the Torah? Aside from the obvious answer that the one who has asked him was a Torah scholar and expected such an answer, I can think of three others:

- Yeshua himself had stated that the Law and Prophets were still in effect (Matthew 5:17-19; Luke 16:16-17).
- Yeshua declared that the words he spoke were the words the Father gave him, and that he never did anything unless he first saw the Father doing it (John 5:19, 14:10, 24).

- Had he instituted anything new or different from what the Father had established, Yeshua would have been guilty of adding to or subtracting from the Word of YHVH, which is a sin according to Torah (Deuteronomy 4:1-2, 12:32, Proverbs 30:6, Revelation 22:18-19).

Thus when we find Yeshua giving a "new commandment" to his disciples, it is not really new, but renewed, or reemphasized:

> A new commandment I give to you, that you love one another, even as I have loved you, that you also love one another. By this all men will know that you are My disciples, if you have love for one another. (John 13:34-35; see also John 15:12-17)

What is the proof of loving God and loving one another? Not merely mental agreement with the Bible or saying a prayer to "receive Jesus into my heart," but actually doing what God said to do. This is not the means of salvation, but the proof of it, as Yeshua himself said:

> **If you love Me, you will keep My commandments**. . . He who has My commandments and keeps them is the one who loves Me; and he who loves Me will be loved by My Father, and I will love him and will disclose Myself to him." Judas (not Iscariot) said to Him, "Lord, what then has happened that You are going to disclose Yourself to us and not to the world?" Jesus answered and said to him, "**If anyone loves Me, he will keep My word; and My Father will love him, and We will come to him and make Our abode with him.** He who does not love Me does not keep My words; and the word which you hear is not Mine, but the Father's who sent Me. (John 15:15, 21-24, emphasis added)

Remember what the Father said at Mount Sinai? "Now then, if you will indeed obey My voice and keep My covenant, then you shall be My own possession among all the peoples. . . ." (Exodus 19:5).

Remember what the people answered? "All that the LORD has spoken we will do!" (Exodus 19:8)

The scene was reenacted at Yeshua's Last Supper with the men he had picked to help him reestablish the lost House of Israel (Matthew 10:1-6, 15:24).

This was the apostolic expectation of the New Covenant. Redemption could not happen to a people who had never been God's possession in the first place, but it could happen to a people who had forsaken YHVH's Covenant and sold themselves to foreign gods. Such was the indictment of the Holy One against his people. The lengthy list of charges appears in 2 Kings 17, concluding with this sentence of judgment:

> So the LORD was very angry with Israel and removed them from His sight; none was left except the tribe of Judah. Also Judah did not keep the commandments of the LORD their God, but walked in the customs which Israel had introduced. The LORD rejected all the descendants of Israel and afflicted them and gave them into the hand of plunderers, until He had cast them out of His sight. When He had torn Israel from the house of David, they made Jeroboam the son of Nebat king. Then Jeroboam drove Israel away from following the LORD and made them commit a great sin. The sons of Israel walked in all the sins of Jeroboam which he did; they did not depart from them until the LORD removed Israel from His sight, as He spoke through all His servants the prophets. So Israel was carried away into exile from their own land to Assyria until this day. (2 Kings 17:18-23)

Here we see the measure of mercy God would have on Judah, but the judgment of utter destruction he inflicted on Israel, just as prophesied by Hosea (Hosea 1:6-7).

Judah, of course, received punishment in Babylon, but the difference is this: Judah repented and returned to the Torah, but Israel/Ephraim never did. As we have seen, Judah's repentance occurred in the prayer of Daniel, the eunuch of the royal seed of David (Daniel 9), followed by national repentance in the days of Ezra and Nehemiah.

Unrepentant Ephraim, however, had no chance for national repentance once they were dispersed among the Gentiles (nations).

God himself had to go running after them. That was a key part of Yeshua's mission, as he explained on more than one occasion. There is no doubt that Yeshua came to be the Messiah for both Judah and Ephraim; both needed the redemption made possible by his atoning death and resurrection. The fact that Yeshua and his disciples were Jewish speaks to the reason his Messianic ministry happened among the Jewish people. The Jewish people alone had the most complete revelation of God; the "oracles of God," as Paul wrote (Romans 3:1). They would understand the redemption offered through Messiah Son of David, and those who received that redemption would become his first witnesses. Paul wrote of that as well:

> For I am not ashamed of the gospel, for it is the power of God for salvation to everyone who believes, **to the Jew first and also to the Greek.** For in it *the* righteousness of God is revealed from faith to faith; as it is written, "BUT THE RIGHTEOUS *man* SHALL LIVE BY FAITH." (Romans 1:16-17, emphasis added)
>
> *There will be* tribulation and distress for every soul of man who does evil, **of the Jew first and also of the Greek**, but glory and honor and peace to everyone who does good, **to the Jew first and also to the Greek**. For there is no partiality with God. For all who have sinned without the Law will also perish without the Law, and all who have sinned under the Law will be judged by the Law; for *it is* not the hearers of the Law *who* are just before God, but the doers of the Law will be justified. (Romans 2:9-13, emphasis added)

## Healing the Sin-Sick Soul

This testimony by Yeshua's witnesses from among the House of Judah has been reignited in our day through the birth of the Messianic Judaism. It should be no surprise that the Torah Awakening among Christians is largely the fruit of the faithful testimony of Messianic Jewish messengers in bringing to light the Jewish, or Hebrew, roots of the Christian faith.

Two thousand years ago, there was no Christian faith; only a Jewish nation clinging to Torah as they understood it in the midst of a pagan world. The Jewish witnesses had to go out into that pagan world and awaken the dispersed remnant of Ephraim, bringing them back into fellowship with the Creator so that they could, in turn, reach the nations with this message of redemption.

There is a high degree of irony throughout this story. The House of Judah had the Torah and understanding of the Covenant, but for some reason did not receive God's Messiah. Although many thousands of Jews, including many priests in the Temple, did become followers of Yeshua (Acts 6:7, 21:20-21), the nation as a whole did not. This, however, did not deter Yeshua from his mission to "seek and to save that which was lost." (Luke 19:10) He expounded on this at one point in his ministry:

> When the scribes of the Pharisees saw that He was eating with the sinners and tax collectors, they said to His disciples, "Why is He eating and drinking with tax collectors and sinners?" And hearing *this*, Jesus said to them, **"*It is* not those who are healthy who need a physician, but those who are sick; I did not come to call the righteous, but sinners."** (Mark 2:16-17, emphasis added)

Who was sick? Who was a sinner? Both Houses of Israel, of course. Only a remnant of the Jewish part of the nation had returned from the Babylonian exile. By the time Yeshua spoke these words, they had been back in the Land for over five centuries and had returned to the Torah, although not perfectly. As we see in the gospel accounts, Yeshua had much to say about the way the religious leaders had added to and twisted the commandments of God. He also had much to say about the barriers those same leaders had erected to prevent sinners from coming into the Kingdom (see especially Matthew 23). Nevertheless, he did ratify their position of authority and what they were supposed to do when he said,

> The scribes and the Pharisees have seated themselves in the chair of Moses; therefore all that they tell you, do and observe, but do not do according to their deeds; for they say *things* and do not do *them*. (Matthew 23:2-3)

What were these religious leaders to do? Teach the Law as Moses taught it! Help the people prove their love for YHVH by doing what he said. Yet the record of the Apostolic Writings indicates the religious leadership of the day continued to act in ways that had brought the prophetic indictment from Jeremiah centuries earlier:

> How can you say, "We are wise, and the law of the LORD is with us"? But behold, the lying pen of the scribes has made *it* into a lie. The wise men are put to shame, they are dismayed and caught; behold, they have rejected the word of the LORD, and what kind of wisdom do they have? Therefore I will give their wives to others, their fields to new owners; because from the least even to the greatest everyone is greedy for gain; from the prophet even to the priest everyone practices deceit. They heal the brokenness of the daughter of My people superficially, saying, "Peace, peace," but there is no peace. (Jeremiah 8:8-11)

And yet, even with such shortcomings, Judah walked out a very important prophetic destiny that involved carrying the scepter or rod of the Torah in administering the spiritual mandate Jacob spoke over him and the House called by his name (Genesis 49:10). Ironically, Jacob's blessing was one of the causes of the enmity and wall of partition between the two parts of the House of Jacob (Isaiah 11:11-13; Ephesians 2:15). As Paul explains, the Torah (Law) provides knowledge of sin, although it cannot bring justification from sin:

> Now we know that whatever the Law says, it speaks to those who are under the Law, so that every mouth may be closed and all the world may become accountable to God; because by the works of the Law no flesh will be justified in His sight; for through the Law *comes* the knowledge of sin. (Romans 3:19-20)

The Torah points us to Messiah (Romans 10:4), and that speaks to the other part of Judah's prophetic destiny: producing the Messiah (Genesis 49:8-10; John 4:22). The Messiah who ministered in and to Judah during his days on earth never lost sight of his purpose to redeem not only Judah, but Judah's brother Ephraim as well. Both were sick of a spiritual malady that required the attention of a Divine Physician. Jeremiah also had something to say about that:

> My sorrow is beyond healing, my heart is faint *within me*! **Behold, listen! The cry of the daughter of my people from a distant land**: "Is the LORD not in Zion? Is her King not within her?"
> "Why have they provoked Me with their graven images, with foreign idols?"
> "Harvest is past, summer is ended, and we are not saved."
> For the brokenness of the daughter of my people I am broken; I mourn, dismay has taken hold of me. **Is there no balm in Gilead? Is there no physician there? Why then has not the health of the daughter of my people been restored?** (Jeremiah 8:18-22, emphasis added)

This is another passage that applies to both Houses, but consider the references to Ephraim's condition. In Yeshua's day, as in ours, he was the sick and hopeless exile who needed help coming home. The healing apparently was not in Gilead, the region beyond Jordan where tribes of the House of Israel had dwelt (Numbers 32). Neither was it in the foreign lands where Ephraim had been scattered. There Ephraim lived out the parable of the Prodigal who had squandered his father's estate and awakened to find himself fallen far below the lofty place he had once known in his father's house.

## TWO ANGRY BROTHERS, PART 2:
## SIMEON

Gustave Doré, "The Prodigal Son," *Doré Bible Gallery*.

Simeon's angry tendencies led his tribe in the opposite direction of Levi's holy pursuits. In the idolatrous rebellion at Baal-peor, the man whom Phinehas killed was none other than Zimri, a Simeonite chief. Thus, while the Levites were defending the honor of the Lord and preserving the distinction between the holy and the profane, the Simeonites led the way in defiling the people and the Name of God in the pursuit of their own passions and lusts (Numbers 25:1-15).

The execution of Zimri may have caused insurmountable offense. At Sinai, Simeon numbered 59,300 fighting men, but 40 years later, the number had diminished to 22,200 – the smallest of all the tribes (Numbers 1:22-23; 26:12-14). Perhaps the drastic loss of population was due to many of the tribe leaving the nation even as their brethren were on the verge of entering the Promised Land.

Simeon is not mentioned in the blessing of Moses in Deuteronomy 33, but is in the list of tribes given land in the Messianic Kingdom (Ezekiel 48), and among the 144,000 taken from all the tribes in Revelation 7. From this we can surmise that something happens to redeem Simeon. Luke 2 may give us a hint at that redemptive action. In the account of righteous Simeon and Anna greeting the infant Messiah Yeshua in the Temple, Luke identifies Anna as from the tribe of Asher, but gives no tribal affiliation for Simeon. Perhaps the old man's name is a clue. Upon recognizing the Messiah, he says:

Now Lord, You are releasing Your bond-servant to depart in peace, according to Your word; for my eyes have seen Your salvation, which You have prepared in the presence of all peoples, A Light of revelation to the Gentiles, and the glory of Your people Israel. (Luke 2:29-32)

Could old Simeon's proclamation be taken to mean that the tribe whose name he bears has come to terms with its anger and offense? We do not know for sure, but we do see that in announcing the presence of Messiah, Simeon, like Phinehas, can enjoy God's covenant of peace.

# 8

# APOSTOLIC EXPECTATIONS, PART 2: THE GOSPEL OF THE KINGDOM

**Restoring the Tree**

If the nations are to see and hear the redemptive blessing of the Covenant Nation of Israel, then Ephraim must be restored to health and reconnected somehow to Judah. That is the reason behind Yeshua's seemingly harsh answer to a desperate Canaanite mother:

> Jesus went away from there, and withdrew into the district of Tyre and Sidon. And a Canaanite woman from that region came out and *began* to cry out, saying, "Have mercy on me, Lord, Son of David; my daughter is cruelly demon-possessed." But He did not answer her a word. And His disciples came and implored Him, saying, "Send her away, because she keeps shouting at us." **But He answered and said, "I was sent only to the lost sheep of the house of Israel."** But she came and *began* to bow down before Him, saying, "Lord, help me!" And He answered and said, "It is not good to take the children's bread and throw it to the dogs." But she said, "Yes, Lord; but even the dogs feed on the crumbs which fall from their masters' table." Then Jesus said to her, "O woman, your faith is great; it shall be done for you as you wish." And her daughter was healed at once. (Matthew 15:21-28, emphasis added)

This "Gentile dog" recognized the Messiah who would one day bring redemption to the whole world, but like Yeshua's mother at the wedding in Cana, she placed a request on him before the proper time (John 2:1-11). The time would come when the foreigners could be joined to the Covenant Nation, a message we have already heard through Isaiah:

> "**Also the foreigners who join themselves to the LORD,** to minister to Him, and to love the name of the LORD, to be His servants, every one who keeps from profaning the sabbath and holds fast My covenant; **even those I will bring to My holy mountain and make them joyful in My house of prayer.** Their burnt offerings and their sacrifices will be acceptable on My altar; for My house will be called a house of prayer for all the peoples."
> **The Lord GOD, who gathers the dispersed of Israel, declares, "Yet *others* I will gather to them, to those *already* gathered."** (Isaiah 56:6-8, emphasis added)

But before the foreigners could be gathered, the sons had to be gathered. The foreigners would be grafted in to the tree, but the tree had to be restored first – the tree of Israel/Ephraim, that is. If we can believe Jeremiah, this is to be a restorative miracle far greater than that of the Exodus from Egypt:

> "**Therefore behold, days are coming,**" declares the LORD, "**when it will no longer be said, 'As the LORD lives, who brought up the sons of Israel out of the land of Egypt,' but, 'As the LORD lives, who brought up the sons of Israel from the land of the north and from all the countries where He had banished them.'** For I will restore them to their own land which I gave to their fathers.
> "**Behold, I am going to send for many fishermen,**" **declares the LORD, "and they will fish for them**; and afterwards I will send for many hunters, and they will hunt them from every mountain and every hill and from the clefts of the rocks. For My eyes are on all their ways; they are not hidden from My face, nor is their iniquity concealed from My eyes. I will first doubly repay their iniquity and their sin, because they have polluted My land; they have filled My inheritance with the carcasses of their detestable idols and with their abominations." (Jeremiah 16:14-18, emphasis added. See also Jeremiah 23:7-8)

I recall learning in church that Yeshua commissioned his disciples to be "fishers of men" (Matthew 4:19, Mark 1:17), but I never learned the reason. Now I know: the fishers went on orders from the Messiah **to gather the scattered exiles of Israel**.

"Scattered exiles" aptly describes both Israel and Judah. How can we know that Yeshua's disciples understood him to mean the House of Israel? That requires a bit of linguistic investigation that takes us back to Jacob's blessing of Joseph's sons, Ephraim and Manasseh:

> He blessed Joseph, and said, "The God before whom my fathers Abraham and Isaac walked, the God who has been my shepherd all my life to this day, the angel who has redeemed me from all evil, bless the lads; and may my name live on in them, and the names of my fathers Abraham and Isaac; and **may they grow into a multitude in the midst of the earth**." (Genesis 48:16, emphasis added)

The Hebrew phrase translated as "grow into a multitude" is *v'yidgu l'rov* (וְיִדְגּוּ לָרֹב), which literally means *multiply like fish*. No wonder Yeshua called fishermen as his core group of disciples!

A second witness to Yeshua's mission to gather the exiles comes from a hostile source: none other than Caiaphas, the high priest who presided over Yeshua's trial. As John relates:

> But one of them, Caiaphas, who was high priest that year, said to them, "You know nothing at all, nor do you take into account that it is expedient for you that one man die for the people, and that the whole nation not perish." Now he did not say this on his own initiative, but being high priest that year, he prophesied that Jesus was going to die for the nation, and not for the nation only, but **in order that He might also gather together into one the children of God who are scattered abroad**. (John 11:49-52, emphasis added)

For the same reason, Yeshua referred to himself as the Good Shepherd in John 10. As he addressed his Jewish audience, he made another of his puzzling statements:

> I have other sheep, which are not of this fold; I must bring them also, and they will hear My voice; and they will become one flock *with* one shepherd. (John 10:16)

This, too, is something I did not fully understand from my church upbringing. Now I know that the other flock is the House of Israel, the sheep scattered without a shepherd (1 Kings 22:17). When Yeshua says he will gather them and make them one flock with Judah, he is not only restating the promise given to Ezekiel of the Two Sticks coming together, but asserting that he is the one who will fulfill that promise:

> My servant David will be king over them, and they will all have one shepherd; and they will walk in My ordinances and keep My statutes and observe them. (Ezekiel 37:24)

The historical record is clear that the Jewish people were not gathered after Yeshua's death and resurrection. In fact, two disastrous wars with Rome over the next hundred years resulted in the scattering of the House of Judah to a far greater extent than in the aftermath of the Babylonian Conquest. The House of Ephraim, however, began to respond to the good news of salvation in Yeshua, and in a spiritual sense at least was indeed gathered by the Good Shepherd.

## Apostolic Expectations in Context

We can have no doubt that the men and women who followed Yeshua during his earthly ministry understood these things. It is apparent in the writings they left us as the first century progressed. Apparent, that is, now that we have uncovered some of the connections of Yeshua's words and deeds with Isaiah's prophecies of Israel's complete restoration. There are far too many to investigate in the scope of this work. The best I can do is present a few and invite the reader to conduct more investigation. I will start with statements scattered throughout the Apostolic Writings that indicate an expectation of an Israel that included not just the Jewish people, but all the tribes:

But He answered and said, **"I was sent only to the lost sheep of the house of Israel."** (Matthew 15:24, emphasis added)

And Jesus said to them, "Truly I say to you, that you who have followed Me, in the regeneration **when the Son of Man will sit on His glorious throne, you also shall sit upon twelve thrones, judging the twelve tribes of Israel**. (Matthew 19:28, emphasis added)

**I have other sheep, which are not of this fold**; I must bring them also, and they will hear My voice; and they will become one flock with one shepherd. (John 10:16, emphasis added)

So when they had come together, they were asking Him, saying, **"Lord, is it at this time You are restoring the kingdom to Israel?"** (Acts 1:6, emphasis added)

And now I [Paul] am standing trial for the hope of the promise made by God to our fathers; **the promise to which our twelve tribes hope to attain**, as they earnestly serve God night and day. And for this hope, O King, I am being accused by Jews. (Acts 26:6-7, emphasis added)

James, a bond-servant of God and of the Lord Jesus Christ, **to the twelve tribes who are dispersed abroad**: Greetings. (James 1:1, emphasis added)

And I heard the number of those who were sealed, one hundred and forty-four thousand sealed **from every tribe of the sons of Israel**: (Revelation 7:4, emphasis added)

And he carried me away in the Spirit to a great and high mountain, and showed me the holy city, Jerusalem, coming down out of heaven from God, having the glory of God. Her brilliance was like a very costly stone, as a stone of crystal-clear jasper. **It had a great and high wall, with twelve gates, and at the gates twelve angels; and names were written on them, which are the names of the twelve tribes of the sons of Israel.** (Revelation 21:10-12, emphasis added)

These are only the references with clear mention of an Israel encompassing both Houses and all the tribes. The real investigative work comes when one takes the Tanakh references the Apostles incorporated in their writings and studies them in context. As we have seen, they may have used only small excerpts ("sound bites" as one might say), but they knew the context of those excerpts, and so did their audiences.

Those references quite often come from passages associated with the exile and restoration of one or both of Israel's Two Houses. For nearly two thousand years, the church has missed the full significance of these references, largely because few have bothered to investigate them and find out, for example, why Matthew chose to quote from Hosea 11 to prove that Yeshua's early childhood in Egypt was a fulfillment of messianic prophecy. It is equally useful to investigate why Paul not only quoted from Hosea, but also drew from Moses in his great exposition on salvation in Romans:

> What if God, although willing to demonstrate His wrath and to make His power known, endured with much patience vessels of wrath prepared for destruction? And *He did so* to make known the riches of His glory upon vessels of mercy, which He prepared beforehand for glory, *even* us, whom He also called, not from among Jews only, but also from among Gentiles. As He says also in Hosea,
> "I WILL CALL THOSE WHO WERE NOT MY PEOPLE, 'MY PEOPLE,' AND HER WHO WAS NOT BELOVED, 'BELOVED.'"
> "AND IT SHALL BE THAT IN THE PLACE WHERE IT WAS SAID TO THEM, 'YOU ARE NOT MY PEOPLE,' THERE THEY SHALL BE CALLED SONS OF THE LIVING GOD." (Romans 9:22-26; quoting Hosea 1:10 and 2:23)

> For Moses writes that the man who practices the righteousness which is based on law shall live by that righteousness. But the righteousness based on faith speaks as follows: "DO NOT SAY IN YOUR HEART, 'WHO WILL ASCEND INTO HEAVEN?' (that is, to bring Christ down), or 'WHO WILL DESCEND INTO THE ABYSS?' (that is, to bring Christ up from the dead)." But what does it say? "THE WORD IS NEAR YOU, IN YOUR MOUTH AND IN YOUR HEART"—that is, the word of

faith which we are preaching, that if you confess with your mouth Jesus *as* Lord, and believe in your heart that God raised Him from the dead, you will be saved; for with the heart a person believes, resulting in righteousness, and with the mouth he confesses, resulting in salvation. For the Scripture says, "WHOEVER BELIEVES IN HIM WILL NOT BE DISAPPOINTED." For there is no distinction between Jew and Greek; for the same *Lord* is Lord of all, abounding in riches for all who call on Him; for "WHOEVER WILL CALL ON THE NAME OF THE LORD WILL BE SAVED." (Romans 10:5-13; with reference to Deuteronomy 30:12, 14)

Paul's reference to Deuteronomy is from the most explicit prophecy Moses spoke about Israel's return from exile. Here it is in context:

> **So it shall be when all of these things have come upon you, the blessing and the curse which I have set before you, and you call *them* to mind in all nations where the LORD your God has banished you, and you return to the LORD your God and obey Him with all your heart and soul according to all that I command you today, you and your sons, then the LORD your God will restore you from captivity, and have compassion on you, and will gather you again from all the peoples where the LORD your God has scattered you.** If your outcasts are at the ends of the earth, from there the LORD your God will gather you, and from there He will bring you back. The LORD your God will bring you into the land which your fathers possessed, and you shall possess it; and He will prosper you and multiply you more than your fathers.
>
> **Moreover the LORD your God will circumcise your heart and the heart of your descendants, to love the LORD your God with all your heart and with all your soul, so that you may live.** The LORD your God will inflict all these curses on your enemies and on those who hate you, who persecuted you. **And you shall again obey the LORD, and observe all His commandments which I command you today.** Then the LORD your God will prosper you abundantly in all the work of your hand, in the offspring of your body

and in the offspring of your cattle and in the produce of your ground, for the LORD will again rejoice over you for good, just as He rejoiced over your fathers; if you obey the LORD your God to keep His commandments and His statutes which are written in this book of the law, if you turn to the LORD your God with all your heart and soul. **For this commandment which I command you today is not too difficult for you, nor is it out of reach.** <u>It is not in heaven, that you should say, "Who will go up to heaven for us to get it for us and make us hear it, that we may observe it?" Nor is it beyond the sea, that you should say, "Who will cross the sea for us to get it for us and make us hear it, that we may observe it?" But the word is very near you, in your mouth and in your heart, that you may observe it.</u> (Deuteronomy 30:1-14, emphasis added) [1]

Why would the apostle link salvation in Yeshua to the return of Israel's exiles, the New Covenant circumcision of the heart, and

---

[1] The observant reader will notice differences in the wording between the texts in Romans 10 and Deuteronomy 30. There is a straightforward explanation for this. First, the verses from Deuteronomy are a direct translation from the Hebrew Masoretic text into English. The passage in Romans comes from the Septuagint, the ancient translation of the Tanakh from Hebrew into Greek. Two centuries before Yeshua's birth, 70 Jewish scholars translated the scriptures into Greek for the benefit of Jews scattered throughout the Greek-speaking world. "Septuagint" refers to the number of translators, which is why the common abbreviation of Septuagint is the Roman numeral LXX (70). As part of the Jewish community in the nations, Paul used the LXX. That is why his words are not exactly the same as those from the direct translation of Deuteronomy.

A second factor is Paul's own interpretive work. The greatest difference concerns the phrase, "Who will descend into the abyss," according to Romans, and "Who will cross the sea," according to Deuteronomy. Both the Masoretic text and the LXX use the words for sea – *yam* (יָם) in Hebrew, *thalassa* (θάλασσα) in Greek. Paul, however, uses the Greek word *abyssos* (ἄβυσσος), from which we get the English word abyss. Although the words are different, the figurative meaning is the same. "Abyss" can mean a cavernous deep, both literally (a canyon or gorge) and figuratively (hell, hades), but it can also refer to the depths of the sea. In fact, some English translations (KJV and NIV, for example) use "deep" instead of "abyss" in Romans 10:7. Considering Paul's point of explaining the atoning work of Messiah, his use of *abyssos* is appropriate as he draws from Torah to make support his reasoning.

obedience to the commandments? For the same reason Peter linked salvation to the promises given through Moses and Hosea:

> But you are A CHOSEN RACE, A royal PRIESTHOOD, A HOLY NATION, A PEOPLE FOR *God's* OWN POSSESSION, so that you may proclaim the excellencies of Him who has called you out of darkness into His marvelous light; for you once were NOT A PEOPLE, but now you are THE PEOPLE OF GOD; you had NOT RECEIVED MERCY, but now you have RECEIVED MERCY. (1 Peter 2:9-10; quoting Hosea 1:10 and Exodus 19:5-6)

Since Peter quotes the exact words YHVH used when he established the Covenant with Israel on Mount Sinai (Exodus 19:5-6), and since he and Paul both refer to Hosea's promise that the House of Israel will be changed from "not a people" to "the people of God," it would seem that they link Yeshua's redemptive work with the restoration of the House of Israel to the Covenant. This is a vital prerequisite to salvation of all the nations: if the Holy Nation is not made whole, then no nation can be made whole.

## Restoring the Kingdom According to Acts 15

This must have been on the mind of James, Yeshua's brother, when he made his famous proclamation recorded in Acts 15. As that chapter relates,

> Some men came down from Judea and *began* teaching the brethren, "Unless you are circumcised according to the custom of Moses, you cannot be saved." (Acts 15:1)

It is unclear whether these particular Jewish emissaries believed Yeshua to be the Messiah, but it is clear that they believed these Gentiles should convert to Judaism. That is the meaning of their statement, "Unless you are circumcised according to the custom of Moses, you cannot be saved." In other words, their expectation, like the expectations of many Jews today, was that the Lost Tribes would have to become Jewish if they were to be restored to the nation.

Paul and Barnabas did not agree with that assessment. Acts 15:2 says they had "great dissension and debate" with these men, and then went to Jerusalem as representatives of the congregation in Galatia to ask the Apostles and Elders for their judgment on the matter. We have great insight into Paul's mind on this issue; it is the reason he wrote the book of Galatians. His letter is not, as many Christian teachers assert, a treatise against the Law, but a warning to these non-Jewish believers that they should not convert to Judaism. The Gospel of the Kingdom that Paul and the other Apostles taught maintained that these Gentiles were united with Israel by virtue of their faith in Yeshua. That much is true regardless whether the non-Jewish believers were descendants of the House of Israel, or foreigners. The Apostles must also have instilled in them an expectation that one day they would be reunited with Judah and restored to the Promised Land under the blissful reign of Messiah Son of David. The temptation, then, would be to shortcut the process by becoming Jews – a shortcut that would be disastrous for them:

> Behold I, Paul, say to you that if you receive circumcision, Christ will be of no benefit to you. And I testify again to every man who receives circumcision, that he is under obligation to keep the whole Law. You have been severed from Christ, you who are seeking to be justified by law; you have fallen from grace. For we through the Spirit, by faith, are waiting for the hope of righteousness. For in Christ Jesus neither circumcision nor uncircumcision means anything, but faith working through love. (Galatians 5:2-6)

When the apostle writes "circumcision," he is referring to the process of conversion to Judaism, not the physical act of circumcision as a sign of the Covenant.[2] What concerns him is that

---

[2] Henry Halley describes circumcision as, "the Initiatory Rite into Judaism." J.K. McKee explains further in his *Galatians for the Practical Messianic*, citing additional references to demonstrate how "circumcision" in Paul's day meant not merely the surgical procedure of circumcision, but the entire process of conversion to Judaism. When we understand this, we realize that when Paul says circumcision "is nothing, and uncircumcision is nothing," he is not contradicting Torah by saying circumcision is no longer a valid sign of the Covenant, but rather is saying that one's status as Jew or as a non-Jew means nothing in the Kingdom context. In other words, "There is neither Jew nor Greek, there is neither slave nor free man, there is neither male nor female; for you are all one in Christ Jesus" (Galatians 3:28). Henry Halley, "Galatians," in *Halley's Bible*

these "returning Ephraimites" were being enticed to "switch sticks" and move from Ephraim to Judah. Paul understood that the full Kingdom restoration required both Houses to be reunited in their unique characteristics, not that one House should become exactly like the other, or that one should absorb the other. Judah cannot become Ephraim, and Ephraim cannot become Judah. Otherwise, the Kingdom remains broken, fragmented, and incomplete. That is why Paul wrote in another letter to non-Jewish believers:

> Only, as the Lord has assigned to each one, as God has called each, in this manner let him walk. And so I direct in all the churches. Was any man called *when he was already* circumcised [already Jewish]? He is not to become uncircumcised. Has anyone been called in uncircumcision [not Jewish]? He is not to be circumcised. **Circumcision is nothing, and uncircumcision is nothing, but *what matters is* the keeping of the commandments of God. Each man must remain in that condition in which he was called.** (1 Corinthians 7:17-20, emphasis added)

This was the argument Paul took with him to Jerusalem. After hearing all the debate, James delivered the final opinion:

> After they had stopped speaking, James answered, saying, "Brethren, listen to me. Simeon has related how God first concerned Himself about taking from among the Gentiles a people for His name. With this the words of the Prophets agree, just as it is written,
> 'AFTER THESE THINGS I WILL RETURN, AND I WILL REBUILD THE TABERNACLE OF DAVID WHICH HAS FALLEN, AND I WILL REBUILD ITS RUINS, AND I WILL RESTORE IT, SO THAT THE REST OF MANKIND MAY SEEK THE LORD, AND ALL THE GENTILES WHO ARE CALLED BY MY NAME,' SAYS THE LORD, WHO MAKES THESE THINGS KNOWN FROM LONG AGO.

---

*Handbook: An Abbreviated Bible Commentary*, 24th ed. (Grand Rapids, Michigan: Zondervan, 1965), 608; John Kimball McKee, "Introduction," in *Galatians for the Practical Messianic* (Richardson, TX: TNN Press, 2012), Kindle.

> Therefore it is my judgment that we do not trouble those who are turning to God from among the Gentiles, but that we write to them that they abstain from things contaminated by idols and from fornication and from what is strangled and from blood. **For Moses from ancient generations has in every city those who preach him, since he is read in the synagogues every Sabbath."** (Acts 15:13-21, emphasis added)

Why would James include that strange tag line at the end of his speech about Moses being taught in the synagogues? It makes sense if he believed the New Covenant involved a circumcision of the heart so the new believers could learn and live by the Torah. That is why the four requirements he specified for the non-Jewish believers all came straight from the heart of the Torah (Leviticus 17:1-20:27). These things would indicate the change of heart and lifestyle expected of one who had encountered the Living God. Moreover, they would be the minimum requirements to make them able to fellowship with Torah keepers (particularly Jews) and begin learning the oracles of God.

That much is clear, but why does James quote from the prophet Amos to support his case? Perhaps we should look at that passage in context as well:

> "Are you not as the sons of Ethiopia to Me, O sons of Israel?" declares the LORD. "Have I not brought up Israel from the land of Egypt, and the Philistines from Caphtor and the Arameans from Kir? Behold, the eyes of the Lord GOD are on the sinful kingdom, and I will destroy it from the face of the earth; nevertheless, I will not totally destroy the house of Jacob," declares the LORD. For behold, I am commanding, and **I will shake the house of Israel among all nations** as *grain* is shaken in a sieve, but not a kernel will fall to the ground. All the sinners of My people will die by the sword, those who say, 'The calamity will not overtake or confront us.'
> 
> **"In that day I will raise up the fallen booth of David, and wall up its breaches; I will also raise up its ruins and rebuild it as in the days of old; that they may possess the**

**remnant of Edom and all the nations who are called by My name," declares the L**ORD **who does this.**

"Behold, days are coming," declares the LORD, "When the plowman will overtake the reaper and the treader of grapes him who sows seed; when the mountains will drip sweet wine and all the hills will be dissolved. **Also I will restore the captivity of My people Israel, and they will rebuild the ruined cities and live *in them*;** they will also plant vineyards and drink their wine, and make gardens and eat their fruit. I will also plant them on their land, and they will not again be rooted out from their land which I have given them," says the LORD your God. (Amos 9:7-15, emphasis added)

This, too, is a passage about the exile and return of the House of Israel. In this case, the "booth" or "tabernacle" (*sukkah* (סֻכָּה), Strongs #H5521 in Hebrew) of David refers to the Kingdom united under his rule. That Kingdom, consisting of all the tribes, fell down when the House of Israel rebelled. The record of that account specifies that the tribes under Ephraim's leadership broke their allegiance to the Davidic Dynasty:

When all Israel *saw* that the king did not listen to them, the people answered the king, saying,
"What portion do we have in David?
*We have* no inheritance in the son of Jesse;
To your tents, O Israel!
Now look after your own house, David!"
So Israel departed to their tents. But as for the sons of Israel who lived in the cities of Judah, Rehoboam reigned over them. Then King Rehoboam sent Adoram, who was over the forced labor, and all Israel stoned him to death. And King Rehoboam made haste to mount his chariot to flee to Jerusalem. **So Israel has been in rebellion against the house of David to this day.** (1 Kings 12:16-19, emphasis added)

The key point here is that the House of Israel rebelled against the Son of David. Thus we should not be surprised to see why James considered those from the nations coming to faith in Yeshua as the

House of Israel pledging allegiance once more to the Son of David. The Kingdom was being restored. The question before the Apostles, therefore, was how to be good stewards of the process so that they would not hinder the holy work of the Almighty.[3]

They certainly did not understand the full parameters of that work. That was evident in the fact that they had to ask Yeshua about it just before he returned to his Father: "Lord, is it at this time You are restoring the kingdom to Israel?" (Acts 1:6) Now we can say with certainty that they were expecting not merely a reestablishment of Jewish political independence, but a restoration of the full Kingdom: both Houses, all twelve tribes, and Yeshua Son of David as Messiah-King. Peter referred to this in a sermon he delivered just weeks afterward:

> But the things which God announced beforehand by the mouth of all the prophets, that His Christ would suffer, He has thus fulfilled. **Therefore repent and return, so that your sins may be wiped away, in order that times of refreshing may come from the presence of the Lord; and that He may send Jesus, the Christ appointed for you, whom heaven must receive until *the* period of restoration of all things about which God spoke by the mouth of His holy prophets from ancient time**. (Acts 3:18-21, emphasis added)

What are these "times of refreshing" and "period of restoration" if not the restoration of the Kingdom? We find reference to this in Malachi:

> Remember the law of Moses My servant, *even the* statutes and ordinances which I commanded him in Horeb for all Israel.
> Behold, I am going to send you Elijah the prophet before the coming of the great and terrible day of the LORD. He will restore the hearts of the fathers to *their* children and the

---

[3] There is no direct correlation between the "tabernacle of David" in Amos 9:11 and the tents of Israel in 1 Kings 12:16. The Hebrew word for tents in 1 Kings 12 is *ohel* (אֹהֶל Strongs #H168) not *sukkah*.

hearts of the children to their fathers, so that I will not come and smite the land with a curse. (Malachi 4:4-6)

The "fathers" of Malachi's prophecy are the Patriarchs Abraham, Isaac, and Jacob, the ones with whom God made the Covenant (Leviticus 26:40-43; Acts 3:25). The children had forgotten not only the Covenant, but the fathers as well, It would take an act of Divine intervention in the form of the prophet Elijah to remedy the situation. As Yeshua explained, Elijah had come in the form of John the Baptist (Matthew 11:11-15, 17:9-13), meaning that John operated in the spirit of Elijah just as Malachi had prophesied.

John's message was simple: "Repent, for the kingdom of heaven is at hand." (Matthew 3:2) In other words, "Remember the law of Moses." That message would prepare the way for the Kingdom to receive its King.

Notice that Malachi references two witnesses: Moses and Elijah. Moses is associated with the House of Judah since the Torah which he gave is in the care of Judah. Elijah is associated with the House of Israel. The record of his career in 1 and 2 Kings takes place almost entirely within the borders of Israel's Northern Kingdom, except for his sojourns in Lebanon (1 Kings 17:8 – 19:1) and Mount Sinai (1 Kings 19). Thus we see in Malachi's reference that the Two Witnesses of Judah and Israel are to call the entire Kingdom to repentance. The one cannot operate without the other; Moses requires someone to call the tribes back to Torah, and Elijah requires the Torah as the standard for his call of repentance.

As it was born out in the careers of both men, so it is born out in the careers of both Houses of Israel.

Which brings us back to the apostolic expectations regarding the Two Houses. Although Yeshua did not give them a straightforward answer when they asked if he would restore the Kingdom at that time, he did say this:

> It is not for you to know times or epochs which the Father has fixed by His own authority; but you will receive power when the Holy Spirit has come upon you; and you shall be My witnesses both in Jerusalem, and in all Judea and

Samaria, and even to the remotest part of the earth. (Acts 1:7-8)

His witnesses would testify to the Two Witnesses, first in Jerusalem, then in Judea, the heartland of the House of Judah, and then in Samaria, heartland of the House of Israel. Only then would they carry the message to the ends of the earth, for only then would the Two Witnesses be equipped to carry the message.

The way is now well prepared. It awaits only the proclamation of the full Gospel of the Kingdom as the Apostles taught it.

## THE CASE AGAINST DAN

Samson, of the tribe of Dan, is the most famous of four Nazirites named in the Bible (the other three are Samuel, John the Baptist, and Paul (Judges 13:2-7, 1 Samuel 1:9-11, Luke 1:8-17, Acts 18:18, 21:17-24). He was a reluctant Nazirite; his story in Judges 13-16 features consistent disregard for the Nazirite vow, except for the requirement to keep his hair long (Numbers 6:1-21). As long as he did not cut his hair, God's grace and mercy allowed him to keep his great strength and position of leadership, but when he yielded to Delilah's temptations, Samson lost not only his hair, but also his strength, his sight, and his freedom.

Gustave Doré, "Samson and Delilah," *Doré Bible Gallery*.

In the darkness of a Philistine prison, this blind judge of Israel repented and returned to the Creator. He gave his own life to bring judgment on Israel's enemies (Judges 16:30).

Samson's story contains clues to the mystery of Dan, which alone among the tribes is not listed in Revelation 7 as contributing to the 144,000 witnesses at the end of the age. This may be a consequence of Dan's role in introducing idol worship to Israel (Judges 18). One of the two idolatrous temples of the Northern Kingdom was in the city of Dan, and Dan's tribal religion may have been a a model for the religion Jeroboam commanded Israel to follow (1 Kings 12:26-33).

Yet, Dan receives territory in the Messianic Kingdom (Ezekiel 48:1-2). How can this be? Perhaps the answer is in Jacob's blessing of Dan:

Dan shall judge his people, as one of the tribes of Israel. Dan shall be a serpent in the way, a horned snake in the path, that bites the horse's heels, so that his rider falls backward. For Your salvation I wait, O Lord. (Genesis 49:16-18)

A serpent is a symbol both of death and of life (Genesis 3:14-15, Numbers 21:6-9, John 3:14-15). It may be that Dan has a role in God's judgment of all Israel in the time of Jacob's Trouble (the Tribulation). It may also be that Dan's redemption must wait until that trial is finished and Messiah's Kingdom is established. If so, then that may explain Jacob's cryptic remark, "For Your salvation I wait, O Lord."

# 9

# FINDING ISRAELITE IDENTITY IN THE NEW COVENANT

## When God Invented Nations

Language is a perilous thing. It can unite us, but quite often it does the opposite. That, by the way, was God's intent. We know this from the story in Genesis 11 of how he created the languages of the earth:

> Now the whole earth used the same language and the same words. It came about as they journeyed east, that they found a plain in the land of Shinar and settled there. They said to one another, "Come, let us make bricks and burn *them* thoroughly." And they used brick for stone, and they used tar for mortar. They said, "Come, let us build for ourselves a city, and a tower whose top *will reach* into heaven, and let us make for ourselves a name, otherwise we will be scattered abroad over the face of the whole earth." The LORD came down to see the city and the tower which the sons of men had built. **The LORD said, "Behold, they are one people, and they all have the same language. And this is what they began to do, and now nothing which they purpose to do will be impossible for them. Come, let Us go down and there confuse their language, so that they will not understand one another's speech."** So the LORD scattered them abroad from there over the face of the whole earth; and they stopped building the city. Therefore its name was called Babel, because there the LORD confused the language of the whole earth; and from there the LORD scattered them abroad over the face of the whole earth. (Genesis 11:1-9, emphasis added)

Ever since then that curse of language has been with us. And, by the way, so has the curse of nations.

Curse of nations? Yes, it does seem to be a curse. It seems that the Lord did not intend for humanity to be scattered and separated across the face of the planet in competing factions. Nevertheless, nations were his idea. The story of the Tower of Babel explains why.

You will notice that mankind also had an idea of uniting themselves as one people, but their idea was not the same as the Almighty's. They wanted to be a single, unified power that could challenge YHVH for sovereignty over this planet. Since these people lived in the generations immediately after the Great Flood, we can suppose that some of them harbored a little resentment at God's destruction of the pre-Flood civilization. Maybe they thought they could do things better than their ancestors, perhaps by building a strong defense that could ward off any further Divine intervention in human affairs. Now since our God does not change (Numbers 23:19; I Samuel 15:29; Malachi 3:6; James 1:17; Hebrews 13:8), and since the eternal governing principles of the universe which he established do not change (Psalm 119:44; II Kings 17:37; Matthew 5:18, 24:34-35; Mark 13:31; Luke 21:33), he had to do something about this blatant rebellion. There can only be one God, after all.

The problem with sin is that it seeks to create many gods – in fact, as many as there are human beings on the earth. That is at the heart of Satan's insidious deception spoken to our mother Eve: "For God knows that in the day you eat from it your eyes will be opened, and you will be like God, knowing good and evil." (Genesis 3:5)

Tragically, the way our Creator dealt with the deception before the Flood was to destroy humanity. He had little choice in the matter since all of humanity apparently was united as a single people, most likely under satanic leadership (not unlike the world we are anticipating at the end of this age when Messiah returns). To make sure he did not have to make a complete end of the human race this time around, the Lord God created nations and then scattered them across the earth. If they were divided in language, they would soon be divided in every other imaginable way, and the resultant wars and rumors of wars would ensure that a united human empire could not arise to defy the Living God until the end of days. In the meantime God could go about the process of cultivating his redemptive work in human hearts while they remained in the nations.

That is not the end of the story, of course. Since the nations refused to bow to the Lord God, and refused even to come into his Presence, he decided to go after them. That is why in Genesis 12, the chapter immediately following that story of the Tower of Babel, we read about the man named Abram. We know him as Abraham, the great Patriarch whom God called out of the nations to establish yet another nation in the Land that he, the Creator, had designated. We also know that the nation the Lord established through Abraham and his seed (meaning his descendants) is the nation God Himself called Israel (Genesis 32:28, 35:10). No other nation on earth has that distinction, as the psalmist explains:

> He declares His words to Jacob,
> His statutes and His ordinances to Israel.
> He has not dealt thus with any nation;
> And as for His ordinances, they have not known them.
> Praise the LORD! (Psalm 147:19-20) .

Why did he do it? We learn that from Moses:

> Moses went up to God, and the LORD called to him from the mountain, saying, "Thus you shall say to the house of Jacob and tell the sons of Israel: 'You yourselves have seen what I did to the Egyptians, and *how* I bore you on eagles' wings, and brought you to Myself. **Now then, if you will indeed obey My voice and keep My covenant, then you shall be My own possession among all the peoples, for all the earth is Mine; and you shall be to Me a kingdom of priests and a holy nation.'** These are the words that you shall speak to the sons of Israel." (Exodus 19:3-6, emphasis added)

We should be able to grasp the meaning of "holy nation." Very simply it means the people God himself chose and set apart from all the other nations (Numbers 23:8-9; Deuteronomy 32:8, 33:28).

That is why Israel is special in just about every sense of the word, but what about "kingdom of priests?" What does that mean?

It means that this special, holy nation does exactly for the nations what the priestly tribe of Levi does for Israel: Israel is to perform the priestly function of interceding for the other nations of the earth. Is that not what priests do? They are the ones who know God's ways and live by them, demonstrating by their example how the Creator wants us all to live, and praying for all the nations in the same way Abraham prayed for Sodom (Genesis 18:16-33).

The nation of Israel is the steward of the Holy Land, the place for which God says he cares (Deuteronomy 11:11-12). It is the land of Jerusalem, God's holy city where he placed his very name (Deuteronomy 12:10-11; 1 Kings 8:27-29, 11:36, 14:21). The Temple in Jerusalem is where the nations are to transact their business with the Almighty. That is what we from Isaiah's word that the Temple is to be a "house of prayer for all the peoples" (Isaiah 56:7). It also explains why all the nations are to go up to Jerusalem in the age of Messiah's Kingdom to worship YHVH at the Feast of Tabernacles (Zechariah 14:16-19).

This description only begins to scratch the surface of what a kingdom of priests is and does. In essence, we could say that this holy nation stands as mediators between the Almighty and the other nations. The ultimate mediator, of course, is our new High Priest from the Order of Melchizedek, Yeshua Son of David, the Messiah (Psalm 110:1-7; Hebrews 5:1-6). All the other priests serve the function the Lord defined long ago, as he explains through Ezekiel:

> Moreover, they shall teach My people the difference between the holy and the profane, and cause them to discern between the unclean and the clean. In a dispute they shall take their stand to judge; they shall judge it according to My ordinances. They shall also keep My laws and My statutes in all My appointed feasts and sanctify My sabbaths. (Ezekiel 44:23-24)

Ezekiel is writing about the function of the Levitical priests in Messiah's Millennial Kingdom, when the Temple is restored and the sacrificial worship is again taking place on a daily basis. It is instructive to learn what that means and why Yeshua our Messiah, as the High Priest, will be presiding over those daily sacrifices (Ezekiel 45:13-46:15). That subject is beyond the scope of this book, but it is one of many things which we find in the Bible that clash with our received understanding of what God is doing in this era which is often called the Church Age.

What is also instructive is what happened to the Levitical priesthood in earlier times. Ezekiel relates that they not only failed in their mission to teach the people the difference between the holy and the profane, but led the way in disregarding the Lord's commandments:

> There is a conspiracy of her prophets in her midst like a roaring lion tearing the prey. They have devoured lives; they have taken treasure and precious things; they have made many widows in the midst of her. **Her priests have done violence to My law and have profaned My holy things; they have made no distinction between the holy and the profane, and they have not taught the difference between the unclean and the clean; and they hide their eyes from My sabbaths, and I am profaned among them.** Her princes within her are like wolves tearing the prey, by shedding blood *and* destroying lives in order to get dishonest gain. (Ezekiel 22:25-27, emphasis added)

**The Holy Nation and the New Covenant**

We should ask, what does this have to do with us as New Covenant believers? If we are to believe the Apostle Peter, it has everything to do with us. Listen to his words:

> Therefore, putting aside all malice and all deceit and hypocrisy and envy and all slander, like newborn babies, long for the pure milk of the word, so that by it you may grow in respect to salvation, if you have tasted the kindness of the Lord. And coming to Him as to a living stone which has been rejected by men, but is choice and precious in the sight of God, **you also, as living stones, are being built up**

**as a spiritual house for a holy priesthood**, to offer up spiritual sacrifices acceptable to God through Jesus Christ. For *this* is contained in Scripture: "BEHOLD, I LAY IN ZION A CHOICE STONE, A PRECIOUS CORNER *stone*, AND HE WHO BELIEVES IN HIM WILL NOT BE DISAPPOINTED."

This precious value, then, is for you who believe; but for those who disbelieve, "THE STONE WHICH THE BUILDERS REJECTED, THIS BECAME THE VERY CORNER *stone*," and, "A STONE OF STUMBLING AND A ROCK OF OFFENSE"; for they stumble because they are disobedient to the word, and to this *doom* they were also appointed. **But you are A CHOSEN RACE, A royal PRIESTHOOD, A HOLY NATION, A PEOPLE FOR *God's* OWN POSSESSION, so that you may proclaim the excellencies of Him who has called you out of darkness into His marvelous light; for you once were NOT A PEOPLE, but now you are THE PEOPLE OF GOD; you had NOT RECEIVED MERCY, but now you have RECEIVED MERCY.**

Beloved, I urge you as aliens and strangers to abstain from fleshly lusts which wage war against the soul. **Keep your behavior excellent among the Gentiles**, so that in the thing in which they slander you as evildoers, they may because of your good deeds, as they observe *them*, glorify God in the day of visitation. (1 Peter 2:1-12, emphasis added)

Notice that Peter quotes from Moses and applies the words to believers in Yeshua. It should be clear by now that when I refer to Yeshua, I mean Jesus Christ, the only begotten Son of God, who has come in the flesh for the purpose of redeeming mankind from the curse of sin and death.

This is yet another aspect of language that can divide us. What I have just said is something that divides us from our Jewish brethren. They are, as Paul tells us in Romans 11, blinded to Messiah's identity. This is consistent with Yeshua's testimony of himself. As he explained, knowing his identity is a matter of revelation:

Now when Jesus came into the district of Caesarea Philippi, He was asking His disciples, "Who do people say that the

Son of Man is?" And they said, "Some *say* John the Baptist; and others, Elijah; but still others, Jeremiah, or one of the prophets." He said to them, "But who do you say that I am?" Simon Peter answered, "You are the Christ, the Son of the living God." And Jesus said to him, **"Blessed are you, Simon Barjona, because flesh and blood did not reveal *this* to you, but My Father who is in heaven.** I also say to you that you are Peter, and upon this rock I will build My church [assembly]; and the gates of Hades will not overpower it." (Matthew 16:13-18, emphasis added)

In truth, God's people suffer from a double blindness. Our Jewish brethren are blind to the identity of Messiah, even though they are expecting Messiah to do the very same things we believers in Yeshua expect. Our expectation is that one day the revelation of his identity will come to them just as it has come to us, but until then we take note that they are believing by faith in the promises of God for redemption, just as Abraham, their father and our father, believed. That is why the apostles Paul, Peter, and James can assert with confidence the testimony of Moses that Abraham believed God and it was counted to him for righteousness (Genesis 15:1-6; Romans 4:3, 20-22; Galatians 3:6; James 2:23). For that reason, I am glad to associate with Jews and even call them brethren. Their faith is the same as my faith, for we both expect the same God to do the same redemptive work in humanity for the glory of his Name. The difference is, by the grace of God I now know the *Object* of our faith, and that his Name is Yeshua (Jesus).

But by the same token, I were blind for a long time to something else: my Israelite identity.

## Israelite, But Not Jewish

Hopefully by this point it should be clear that I am not saying that I am Jewish. I am not, nor do I desire to be. Nor am I saying that I know for certain that my ancestors were members of one of Israel's lost tribes (although I have more to say on this in the next chapter). Nevertheless, I affirm my non-Jewish Israelite identity, making that statement in faith in the expectation that Messiah will organize us all into tribes one day.

I make this statement because I carry to the logical conclusion the reasoning Paul lays out in his passages on the commonwealth of Israel, the One New Man, and the grafting of non-Jews into Israel's olive tree. Let us review those passages, beginning with the places where Hosea and Jeremiah identify Israel as an olive tree:

Already we know that Jeremiah 11:15 says Israel is a "green olive tree." What we have not examined is the context of that description. It may be a surprise to learn that he did so in the context of pronouncing judgment on both Houses, but with particular emphasis on Judah:

> Then the LORD said to me, "A conspiracy has been found among the men of Judah and among the inhabitants of Jerusalem. They have turned back to the iniquities of their ancestors who refused to hear My words, and they have gone after other gods to serve them; **the house of Israel and the house of Judah have broken My covenant which I made with their fathers**."
> Therefore thus says the LORD, "Behold I am bringing disaster on them which they will not be able to escape; though they will cry to Me, yet I will not listen to them. Then the cities of Judah and the inhabitants of Jerusalem will go and cry to the gods to whom they burn incense, but they surely will not save them in the time of their disaster. For your gods are as many as your cities, O Judah; and as many as the streets of Jerusalem are the altars you have set up to the shameful thing, altars to burn incense to Baal. **Therefore do not pray for this people, nor lift up a cry or prayer for them; for I will not listen when they call to Me because of their disaster.**
> "What right has My beloved in My house when she has done many vile deeds? Can the sacrificial flesh take away from you your disaster, so *that* you can rejoice?"
> **The LORD called your name, "A green olive tree, beautiful in fruit and form"**; with the noise of a great tumult he has kindled fire on it, and its branches are

worthless. **The LORD of hosts, who planted you, has pronounced evil against you because of the evil of the house of Israel and of the house of Judah**, which they have done to provoke Me by offering up sacrifices to Baal. (Jeremiah 11:9-17, emphasis added)

Those are hardly comforting words, particularly when we recall a catch phrase YHVH's Prophets use regarding the idolatry of both Houses. As we have seen already in Jeremiah 3,

Then the LORD said to me in the days of Josiah the king, "Have you seen what faithless Israel did? She went up on every high hill and under **every green tree**, and she was a harlot there. I thought, 'After she has done all these things she will return to Me'; but she did not return, and her treacherous sister Judah saw it. And I saw that for all the adulteries of faithless Israel, I had sent her away and given her a writ of divorce, yet her treacherous sister Judah did not fear; but she went and was a harlot also. (Jeremiah 3:6-8, emphasis added)

Moses is the first to use the phrase, every green tree, in the context of what the Hebrews should do when they take possession of the Promised Land:

You shall utterly destroy all the places where the nations whom you shall dispossess serve their gods, on the high mountains and on the hills and under **every green tree**. (Deuteronomy 12:2, emphasis added)

In later books, the writers use "every green tree" to describe the idolatry of the people of both Houses and their kings (2 Kings 16:4, 17:10; 2 Chronicles 28:4; Jeremiah 2:20, 3:13; Ezekiel 6:13, 20:47). It is bad enough that they do so under any kind of tree, but when they are the green olive tree planted by the Almighty himself, we understand all the better why he refers to this treacherous tendency as the worst form of marital infidelity. How much worse can it get? We see that in Jeremiah 11. Because Judah continued to act like a prostitute even after having seen the judgment inflicted on Israel, *God forbids the prophet even from praying for the people.*

What hope can there be for a people when YHVH instructs his Prophets that there is no point in interceding for them? And yet this is but the second of three occasions in which the Lord does so for Judah (the others being Jeremiah 7:16 and 14:11). No wonder some have concluded over the centuries that the Jewish people, or the people of Israel as a whole, have no more place in the Covenant of YHVH.

They are, of course, mistaken. The olive tree passage from Hosea is but one scriptural testimony to the endless compassion and faithfulness of a God who keeps his promises even when his people disregard and forget them:

> Return, O Israel, to the LORD your God, for you have stumbled because of your iniquity. Take words with you and return to the LORD. Say to Him, "Take away all iniquity and receive *us* graciously, that we may present the fruit of our lips. Assyria will not save us, we will not ride on horses; nor will we say again, 'Our god,' to the work of our hands; for in You the orphan finds mercy."
> I will heal their apostasy, I will love them freely, for My anger has turned away from them. I will be like the dew to Israel; he will blossom like the lily, and he will take root like *the cedars of* Lebanon. **His shoots will sprout, and his beauty will be like the olive tree** and his fragrance like *the cedars of* Lebanon. Those who live in his shadow will again raise grain, and they will blossom like the vine. His renown *will be* like the wine of Lebanon.
> O Ephraim, what more have I to do with idols? It is I who answer and look after you. I am like a luxuriant cypress; from Me comes your fruit.
> Whoever is wise, let him understand these things; *whoever* is discerning, let him know them. For the ways of the LORD are right, and the righteous will walk in them, but transgressors will stumble in them. (Hosea 14:1-9, emphasis added)

How interesting that the words of comfort and restoration appear here in Hosea, given to Ephraim a full century before Jeremiah delivered his words of judgment to Judah. What do we conclude from this but that the Lord once again declares the end from the beginning? Perhaps, if Judah would not hear the corrective word or take the lesson from the judgment Ephraim suffered, they might at least take comfort in the promise to restore all of Israel one day. That, too, is consistent with YHVH's Covenant promises. Even as he proclaimed through Moses the penalties for breaking the Covenant, he made this declaration:

> Yet in spite of this, when they are in the land of their enemies, I will not reject them, nor will I so abhor them as to destroy them, breaking My covenant with them; for I am the LORD their God. **But I will remember for them the covenant with their ancestors**, whom I brought out of the land of Egypt in the sight of the nations, that I might be their God. I am the LORD. (Leviticus 26:44-45, emphasis added)

What kind of God is this who promises to remember what his people forget? The covenantal amnesia afflicted Ephraim far more grievously than it did Judah, but neither House was immune. Judah, at least, remembered who – and whose – they were. Ephraim, if we may infer from the cultural memories of reemerging Hebrew descendants in many people groups, remembered only that they had offended their God and lost their way.

Paul expressed this condition more delicately, referring to it as a blindness, or a hardening:

> What then? What Israel is seeking, it has not obtained, but those who were chosen obtained it, and the rest were hardened; just as it is written,
> "GOD GAVE THEM A SPIRIT OF STUPOR,
> EYES TO SEE NOT AND EARS TO HEAR NOT,
> DOWN TO THIS VERY DAY."
> And David says,
> "LET THEIR TABLE BECOME A SNARE AND A TRAP,
> AND A STUMBLING BLOCK AND A RETRIBUTION TO THEM.
> "LET THEIR EYES BE DARKENED TO SEE NOT,
> AND BEND THEIR BACKS FOREVER."
> (Romans 11:7-10)

The usual understanding of Romans 9, 10, and 11 is that those chapters comprise an essay in which Paul explains that the Jews still have a place in God's plan, and that they will be restored to his Covenant when the blindness upon them regarding Messiah's identity is removed. How does this relate to what we have learned about non-Jews being joined with Jews (the "Uncircumcision" with the "Circumcision") in the Commonwealth of Israel? If Jews were cut out of the Covenant, then so were the non-Jewish Israelites of Ephraim. How, then, can anyone be brought back into it?

Paul answers that with a passage that takes us back to the olive tree:

> **But if some of the branches were broken off, and you, being a wild olive, were grafted in among them and became partaker with them of the rich root of the olive tree, do not be arrogant toward the branches; but if you are arrogant,** *remember that* **it is not you who supports the root, but the root** *supports* **you.** You will say then, "Branches were broken off so that I might be grafted in." Quite right, they were broken off for their unbelief, but you stand by your faith. Do not be conceited, but fear; for if God did not spare the natural branches, he will not spare you, either. Behold then the kindness and severity of God; to those who fell, severity, but to you, God's kindness, if you continue in His kindness; otherwise you also will be cut off. And they also, if they do not continue in their unbelief, will be grafted in, for God is able to graft them in again. **For if you were cut off from what is by nature a wild olive tree, and were grafted contrary to nature into a cultivated olive tree, how much more will these who are the natural** *branches* **be grafted into their own olive tree?** (Romans 11:17-24, emphasis added)

Who is the olive tree Paul describes here? Is it only the Jews, or is it all of Israel? If it is not all Israel – Judah *and* Ephraim – then we have a serious problem. The church has often interpreted this passage to mean that if Messiah is to make all people one nation ("spiritual Israel"), then the Jews must become Christians. Or perhaps in a contrary view, maybe it means all Christians become Jews. This is the conundrum we face if we continue to believe that Israel consists only of the Jewish people.

But what if we have missed something? This is where we get to the other part of the blindness that has come upon Israel: the blindness that has caused non-Jewish Israel to forget their identity. This blindness has served well to focus our attention on the saving power of Messiah Yeshua, but it has caused confusion not only among Jews and Israelites of Ephraimite stock, but also among the myriad thousands of non-Israelites who have come into the New, or Renewed, Covenant.

**About that New Covenant**

Christians can rightly be called "New Covenant believers." It is the New Covenant, sealed with the blood of Messiah Yeshua, that makes it possible for us to come into fellowship with our Creator (Luke 22:20; 1 Corinthians 11:25). But what exactly is that New Covenant? You will not find it explained in the Gospels. It is fulfilled there, but the explanation appears elsewhere, in the book of Hebrews. Let us read it in its entirety:

> For finding fault with them, He says,
> "BEHOLD, DAYS ARE COMING, SAYS THE LORD, WHEN I WILL EFFECT A NEW COVENANT WITH THE HOUSE OF ISRAEL AND WITH THE HOUSE OF JUDAH; NOT LIKE THE COVENANT WHICH I MADE WITH THEIR FATHERS ON THE DAY WHEN I TOOK THEM BY THE HAND TO LEAD THEM OUT OF THE LAND OF EGYPT; FOR THEY DID NOT CONTINUE IN MY COVENANT, AND I DID NOT CARE FOR THEM, SAYS THE LORD.
> "FOR THIS IS THE COVENANT THAT I WILL MAKE WITH THE HOUSE OF ISRAEL AFTER THOSE DAYS, SAYS THE LORD: I WILL PUT MY LAWS INTO THEIR MINDS, AND I WILL WRITE THEM ON THEIR HEARTS. AND I WILL BE THEIR GOD, AND THEY SHALL BE MY PEOPLE. AND THEY SHALL NOT TEACH EVERYONE HIS FELLOW CITIZEN, AND EVERYONE HIS BROTHER, SAYING, 'KNOW THE LORD,' FOR ALL WILL KNOW ME, FROM THE LEAST TO THE GREATEST OF THEM.

"FOR I WILL BE MERCIFUL TO THEIR INIQUITIES, AND I WILL REMEMBER THEIR SINS NO MORE." (Hebrews 8:8-11)

That is the New Covenant. The first question we should ask is, "With whom is God finding fault?" When you read Hebrews 8 in context, you will see that it is our ancestors of Israel, and specifically the Levitical priesthood, the ones who failed to teach the people the difference between the holy and the profane and how to live righteously according to God's standards.

Interestingly enough, this is the longest quote from the Tanakh that appears in the Apostolic Writings. The author of Hebrews lifts his text from Jeremiah 31. Let us read the original:

> "Behold, days are coming," declares the LORD, "when I will make a new covenant with the house of Israel and with the house of Judah, not like the covenant which I made with their fathers in the day I took them by the hand to bring them out of the land of Egypt, My covenant which they broke, although I was a husband to them," declares the LORD. "But this is the covenant which I will make with the house of Israel after those days," declares the LORD, "I will put My law within them and on their heart I will write it; and I will be their God, and they shall be My people. They will not teach again, each man his neighbor and each man his brother, saying, 'Know the LORD,' for they will all know Me, from the least of them to the greatest of them," declares the LORD, "for I will forgive their iniquity, and their sin I will remember no more." (Jeremiah 31:31-34)[1]

Notice something else about this New Covenant. Who are the parties to it? Is it Jews and Gentiles? Is it Israel and the United States? True, it is two groups of people, but it is not what you

---

[1] Once again we see differences in translation between the Tanakh and the Apostolic Writings. The writer of Hebrews, like Paul, used the Greek Septuagint (LXX) when quoting from Jeremiah, while the English translators of the Tanakh looked directly to the Hebrew of the Masoretic text. The words in Hebrews are not exactly the same as those from the direct translation of Jeremiah, but the essential meaning is still there. In other words, the terms used simply reflect the difference in perspective of translators separated by several centuries and cultures.

would expect. The text says, *"a new covenant with the House of Israel and with the House of Judah."*

This brings us to a fundamental principle we did not understand in our church upbringing. It simply was not on our radar, even though, like so many mysteries of God, it has always been right there in plain sight. The New Covenant clearly speaks to the two parts of the nation of Israel: the Jewish part (House of Judah), and the non-Jewish part (House of Israel). Somehow this New Covenant has something to do with bringing those two halves of the nation back together again.

So how does one get to be part of this New Covenant? That is where our Christian training is of such great value. We enter by faith in Messiah Yeshua, by the grace of YHVH his Father. It is not by works or by any act designed to attain our own righteousness, but by appropriating the free gift of God which Christians call salvation, and which Jews call redemption. Once we attach ourselves to the King of Israel (Yeshua, Son of David and heir to David's throne), then we become his subjects and citizens of his kingdom. That means we become Israelites, regardless of our ancestry.

This can be confusing if one has never considered it before. I did not say I have become Jewish. I said I have become *Israelite*. There is a distinction.

Remember the illustration using the states of the United States of America. Those Americans who live in Texas can be called either Americans, or Texans, but they could not be called New Yorkers because they do not live in and perhaps have never even visited the state of New York.

Now suppose a Texan were to travel to Europe. If on that journey someone asked if he were a New Yorker, he would have to say no. But suppose that the European who had asked the question then said, "But you are an American. Aren't all Americans also New Yorkers?" The visitor from Texas would have to answer, "No, that is not correct. All New Yorkers are Americans, but not all Americans are New Yorkers."

In the same way, as I have said earlier, *all Jews are Israelites, but not all Israelites are Jews.*

I cannot overemphasize this point. What the world has known up to now is a division between Jews and everyone else. "Everyone else" are Gentiles, meaning the people of the nations other than the Jewish nation. What the Lord is clarifying in our understanding today is that the division is not between Jews and Gentiles, but between *Israelites* (*Hebrews*) and Gentiles.

Jews are now and always will be Israelites. They are the visible sign to the world that YHVH is God and that he keeps his promises. They perform that function simply by remaining in existence. Of course, the Jewish people do much more than that, having been entrusted not only with the oracles of God, but also being the people of our Messiah (Genesis 49:10; Romans 3:1-2; John 4:22; Revelation 5:5). However, they are not all there is to the nation of Israel.

The Word of God says that the rest of the nation must be restored one day, joining with the House of Judah to complete the Kingdom of Messiah (Ezekiel 37:15-28). This is where we come in: whether we are physical descendants of the tribes of the Northern Kingdom or not, because we have trusted in our Messiah-King, we become part of the Israelite nation tracing lineage to the Northern Kingdom.

Understand something else: **this is not Replacement Theology**. We Ephraimites, or Hebraic believers, or B'ney Yosef (children of Joseph), or however we will eventually be called, *do not replace the Jewish people as Israel.* Neither do we become Jews. Rather, we join with Jews to contribute our part to a completed nation.

Let us take this one step further: if we deny the truth of our Israelite identity, then we are indeed practicing Replacement Theology, but it is *reverse Replacement Theology*. Saying that no one except Jews can be Israel denies the heritage of millions, even billions, whom scripture says are children of Abraham because they, like our father Abraham, believe the promises of God and therefore through faith obtain righteousness. This is a key point Paul emphasizes in his letter to the Galatians:

For you are all sons of God through faith in Christ Jesus. For all of you who were baptized into Christ have clothed yourselves with Christ. There is neither Jew nor Greek, there is neither slave nor free man, there is neither male nor female; for you are all one in Christ Jesus. **And if you belong to Christ, then you are Abraham's descendants, heirs according to promise.** (Galatians 3:26-29, emphasis added)

To what promise is Paul referring? The eternal promise YHVH made to Abraham:

And He took him outside and said, "Now look toward the heavens, and count the stars, if you are able to count them." And He said to him, "So shall your descendants be." (Genesis 15:5)

This is the promise that brought Abraham's pivotal response:

Then he believed in the LORD; and He reckoned it to him as righteousness. (Genesis 15:6)

As we have seen, Paul and James (James 2:23) both consider this response – belief in the promises of YHVH, and life-changing action based thereon – as the formula common both to Abraham's redemption and to the redemption, the salvation, of all of his descendants, both physical and spiritual. That is why Paul can assert that all who believe on Messiah Yeshua, the instrument by which YHVH's promises are fulfilled, become part of Abraham's seed, and therefore Hebrews.

How can we be so certain of all this? Because the Word of God says so. We could go to many places for confirmation, but let us remain in Jeremiah 31. Perhaps you have never read this chapter in its entirety. Let us do so now and allow the scripture to speak for itself. Listen with your heart, and you will hear some things you never anticipated had anything to do with the New Covenant:

"At that time," declares the LORD, "I will be the God of all the families of Israel, and they shall be My people." Thus says the LORD, "The people who survived the sword found grace in the wilderness—Israel, when it went to find its rest."

The LORD appeared to him from afar, *saying*, "I have loved you with an everlasting love; therefore I have drawn you with lovingkindness. Again I will build you and you will be rebuilt, O virgin of Israel! Again you will take up your tambourines, and go forth to the dances of the merrymakers. Again you will plant vineyards on the hills of Samaria; the planters will plant and will enjoy *them*. **For there will be a day when watchmen on the hills of Ephraim call out, 'Arise, and let us go up *to* Zion, to the LORD our God.'"**

For thus says the LORD, "Sing aloud with gladness for Jacob, and shout among the chief of the nations; proclaim, give praise and say, 'O LORD, save Your people, the remnant of Israel.' **Behold, I am bringing them from the north country, and I will gather them from the remote parts of the earth, among them the blind and the lame, the woman with child and she who is in labor with child, together; a great company, they will return here.** With weeping they will come, and by supplication I will lead them; I will make them walk by streams of waters, on a straight path in which they will not stumble; **for I am a father to Israel, and Ephraim is My firstborn."**

Hear the word of the LORD, O nations, and declare in the coastlands afar off, and say, **"He who scattered Israel will gather him and keep him as a shepherd keeps his flock."** For the LORD has ransomed Jacob and redeemed him from the hand of him who was stronger than he.

"They will come and shout for joy on the height of Zion, and they will be radiant over the bounty of the LORD—over the grain and the new wine and the oil, and over the young of the flock and the herd; and their life will be like a watered garden, and they will never languish again. Then the virgin will rejoice in the dance, and the young men and the old, together, for I will turn their mourning into joy and will comfort them and give them joy for their sorrow. I will fill the soul of the priests with abundance, and My people will be satisfied with My goodness," declares the LORD.

Thus says the LORD, **"A voice is heard in Ramah, lamentation *and* bitter weeping. Rachel is weeping for her children; she refuses to be comforted for her** children, because they are no more." Thus says the LORD, "Restrain your voice from weeping and your eyes from tears; for your work will be rewarded," declares the LORD, "And they will return from the land of the enemy. There is hope for your future," declares the LORD, "And *your* children will return to their own territory. **I have surely heard Ephraim grieving, 'You have chastised me, and I was chastised, like an untrained calf; bring me back that I may be restored, for You are the LORD my God.** For after I turned back, I repented; and after I was instructed, I smote on *my* thigh; I was ashamed and also humiliated because I bore the reproach of my youth.' **Is Ephraim My dear son? Is he a delightful child? Indeed, as often as I have spoken against him, I certainly *still* remember him; therefore My heart yearns for him; I will surely have mercy on him," declares the LORD.**

"Set up for yourself roadmarks, place for yourself guideposts; direct your mind to the highway, the way by which you went. Return, O virgin of Israel, return to these your cities. How long will you go here and there, O faithless daughter? For the LORD has created a new thing in the earth—a woman will encompass a man."

Thus says the LORD of hosts, the God of Israel, "Once again they will speak this word in the land of Judah and in its cities when I restore their fortunes, 'The LORD bless you, O abode of righteousness, O holy hill!' Judah and all its cities will dwell together in it, the farmer and they who go about with flocks. For I satisfy the weary ones and refresh everyone who languishes." At this I awoke and looked, and my sleep was pleasant to me.

**"Behold, days are coming," declares the LORD, "when I will sow the house of Israel and the house of Judah with the seed of man and with the seed of beast.** As I have watched over them to pluck up, to break down, to overthrow, to destroy and to bring disaster, so I will watch over them to build and to plant," declares the LORD. In those days they will not say again, 'The fathers have eaten sour grapes, and the children's teeth are set on edge.' But everyone will die for his own iniquity; each man who eats the sour grapes, his teeth will be set on edge.

"Behold, days are coming," declares the LORD, "when I will make a new covenant with the house of Israel and with the house of Judah, not like the covenant which I made with their fathers in the day I took them by the hand to bring them out of the land of Egypt, My covenant which they broke, although I was a husband to them," declares the LORD. "But this is the covenant which I will make with the house of Israel after those days," declares the LORD, "I will put My law within them and on their heart I will write it; and I will be their God, and they shall be My people. They will not teach again, each man his neighbor and each man his brother, saying, 'Know the LORD,' for they will all know Me, from the least of them to the greatest of them," declares the LORD, "for I will forgive their iniquity, and their sin I will remember no more."

Thus says the LORD, Who gives the sun for light by day and the fixed order of the moon and the stars for light by night, Who stirs up the sea so that its waves roar; the LORD of hosts is His name: "<u>If this fixed order departs from before Me</u>," declares the LORD, "<u>Then the offspring of Israel also will cease from being a nation before Me forever.</u>" Thus says the LORD, "If the heavens above can be measured and the foundations of the earth searched out below, then I will also cast off all the offspring of Israel for all that they have done," declares the LORD.

"Behold, days are coming," declares the LORD, "when the city will be rebuilt for the LORD from the Tower of Hananel to the Corner Gate. The measuring line will go out farther straight ahead to the hill Gareb; then it will turn to Goah. And the whole valley of the dead bodies and of the ashes, and all the fields as far as the brook Kidron, to the corner of the Horse Gate toward the east, shall be holy to the LORD; it will not be plucked up or overthrown anymore forever." (Jeremiah 31:1-40, emphasis added)

Do you see the Gospel of the Kingdom in this New Covenant? It is not some ethereal heavenly kingdom that Jesus came to create out of nothing, but the very real, very spiritual, and very physical Kingdom of Israel which he has come to restore. That is why he tells us to seek first God's Kingdom and his righteousness (Matthew 6:33).

Why is this important? *Because none of the other kingdoms or nations of the earth will survive the coming wrath of the Almighty.* As we have seen, that is something else Jeremiah tells us:

> "But as for you, O Jacob My servant, do not fear, nor be dismayed, O Israel! For, see, I am going to save you from afar, and your descendants from the land of their captivity; and Jacob will return and be undisturbed and secure, with no one making him tremble. O Jacob My servant, do not fear," declares the Lord, "For I am with you. **For I will make a full end of all the nations where I have driven you, yet I will not make a full end of you**; but I will correct you properly and by no means leave you unpunished." (Jeremiah 46:27-28, emphasis added)

He says this also by the Prophet Amos:

> "Behold, the eyes of the Lord God are on the sinful kingdom, and I will destroy it from the face of the earth; nevertheless, I will not totally destroy the house of Jacob," declares the Lord. "For behold, I am commanding, and **I will shake the house of Israel** among all nations as grain is shaken in a sieve, **but not a kernel will fall to the ground**." (Amos 9:8-9)

As we have seen, that passage of Amos contains the same verses the Apostle James cites in the discussion about what to do with the people coming into the Kingdom from among the gentiles:

> "In that day I will raise up the fallen booth [tabernacle] of David, and wall up its breaches; I will also raise up its ruins and rebuild it as in the days of old; that they may possess the remnant of Edom [remnant of mankind] and all the nations who are called by My name," declares the Lord who does this. (Amos 9:11-12; see also Acts 15:13-21)

There is much more to be said about this, but here is the crucial point: *There is no salvation outside of the nation of Israel.*

That is why the Lord made a way for every person, every tribe, every nation, every tongue to join with his people. This is the One New Man, the New Creation which is able to live by the righteous standards of the Holy God because he has created new hearts in those who can receive and walk out his laws, instructions, and commandments (Deuteronomy 10:15-17, 30:1-6; Ezekiel 36:22-32). It meets with his intent to have one unified world and one unified humanity, not according to the vision of any man in rebellion against God, but according to the vision God Himself intended to bring about all along.

Do not take my word alone; examine these things for yourselves. But consider this: if what I have said is indeed the counsel of scripture, then instead of resisting the idea of our shared Israelite identity, we should be proclaiming it from the rooftops.

This is, after all, what we are supposed to do:

> This gospel of the kingdom shall be preached in the whole world as a testimony to all the nations, and then the end will come. (Matthew 24:14)

## Manasseh's Double Portion

Surprisingly, the tribe with the largest territory was neither Judah nor Ephraim, but Manasseh. Joseph's oldest son received Gilead east of the Jordan, as well as territory spanning the distance from the Jordan to the Mediterranean coast, making Manasseh the only tribe whose territory stretched from Israel's eastern border to the sea. This fits the pattern in Jacob's family. Even as Jacob split the inheritance between Judah (the Ruler) and Joseph (the double portion of the Firstborn), Joseph's inheritance was divided between Manasseh, who received a double portion, and Ephraim, who received the blessing of preeminence (Genesis 48:17-19; Numbers 32:33-42; Joshua 13:29-32, 17:1-13).

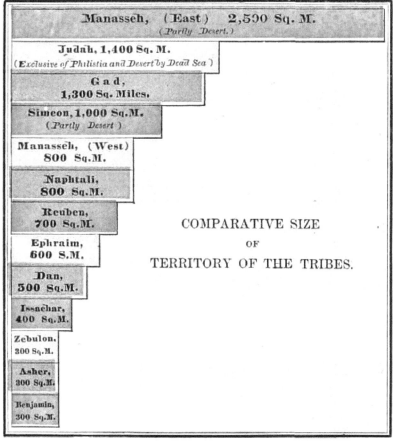

Hurlbut, *Bible Atlas*, 56.

# 10

# ONE SEED

**Avoiding Unprofitable Genealogies**

Among the most valuable lessons we have learned from the church over the last 20 centuries is how to live godly lives. Yeshua and his Apostles provide the examples for us, both in the stories of their lives and in the letters of the Apostles. Paul especially provides good commentary on what constitutes godly behavior for the people and for their leaders. Regarding leaders in the congregations, Paul includes this advice:

> But avoid foolish controversies and genealogies and strife and disputes about the Law, for they are unprofitable and worthless. (Titus 3:9; see also 1 Timothy 1:3-7

It may be that Paul's exhortation to avoid genealogies has contributed to the tendency among Christians to gloss over the tedious lists of names in many Tanakh passages. The first nine chapters of 1 Chronicles, for example, are guaranteed to make the reader wonder why such dry material ever got into the Bible.

The same could be said for the second chapter of Ezra: 70 verses containing a bewildering list of the families included in the first contingent of Jews to return from the Babylonian Captivity in 538 BCE. It makes no sense to the casual reader, and seems counterintuitive when considered in the light of Paul's instruction.

Except that this is not a foolish controversy about an endless genealogy. Ezra's list and the other genealogies throughout scripture testify to something very important: the seed of Abraham is a physical seed, not merely a spiritual concept. If there were no physical continuity to the line of Abraham, Isaac, and Jacob, then the covenantal promises of YHVH would be of no effect.

Thus we have in Ezra's list a crucial record to show that the Jewish people who came back from Babylon were indeed genuine descendants of the House of Judah and the sole extant portion of the nation of Israel. Had those returning exiles been anything other than genuine Israelites, then this promise of God would have been irrelevant:

> And the word of the LORD came to Jeremiah, saying, "Have you not observed what this people have spoken, saying, 'The two families which the LORD chose, He has rejected them'? Thus they despise My people, no longer are they as a nation in their sight. Thus says the LORD, 'If My covenant *for* day and night *stand* not, *and* the fixed patterns of heaven and earth I have not established, then I would reject the descendants of Jacob and David My servant, not taking from his descendants rulers over the descendants of Abraham, Isaac and Jacob. But I will restore their fortunes and will have mercy on them.'" (Jeremiah 33:23-26; see also Jeremiah 31:35-37)

This is a foundational promise. When Paul writes that Yeshua's disciples are grafted into the olive tree of Israel, he is not postulating some vague spiritualized shadow of this promise. Remember who is writing this: Paul, the zealous Torah scholar who defended his conduct as "apostle to the gentiles" (Romans 1:5, 11:13; Galatians 2:8) in Jewish and Roman courts of law with words like these:

> So then, all Jews know my manner of life from my youth up, which from the beginning was spent among my *own* nation and at Jerusalem; since they have known about me for a long time, if they are willing to testify, that I lived *as* a Pharisee according to the strictest sect of our religion. **And now I am standing trial for the hope of the promise made by God to our fathers;** *the promise* **to which our twelve tribes hope to attain, as they earnestly serve** *God* **night and day.** And for this hope, O King, I am being accused by Jews. (Acts 26:4-7, emphasis added)

**How do the Twelve Tribes Return?**

The "hope of the promise made by God" to the twelve tribes is a hope of physical return *and* spiritual regeneration; the one cannot be completed without the other. Thus, with the return of Judah from Babylon, the physical seed had to be documented through the genealogies. To this day, the Jewish people have labored diligently to maintain records of their lineage. That is why the Levitical priesthood can be reconstituted, as the Temple Institute is doing even now.[1] It is also why there are thousands of identifiable descendants of King David still walking this earth, leading to expectations among some Jewish scholars that one of them may someday become ruler of the restored Kingdom.[2] This verifies exactly what God said over 2,500 years ago:

> The word of the LORD came to Jeremiah, saying, "Thus says the LORD, **'If you can break My covenant for the day and My covenant for the night, so that day and night will not be at their appointed time, then My covenant may also be broken with David My servant so that he will not have a son to reign on his throne, and with the Levitical priests, My ministers.** As the host of heaven cannot be counted and the sand of the sea cannot be measured, so I will multiply the descendants of David My servant and the Levites who minister to Me.'" (Jeremiah 33:19-22, emphasis added)

Which brings us back to Ezra's tedious list of the first returnees from Babylon. Near the end we find this interesting note:

---

[1] Hana Levi Julian, "Sons of Aaron – The Priestly Tribe – Convene in Jerusalem", printed from Arutz 7, The Temple Institute, July 16 2007, accessed June 18, 2017, http://www.templeinstitute.org/archive/16-07-07.htm. Zalman Tzorfati, "Training Kohanim in Mitzpeh Yericho," Beis Moschiach, accessed June 18, 2017, http://beismoshiachmagazine.org/articles/training-kohanim-in-mitzpeh-yericho.html.
[2] Adam Eliyahu Berkowitz, "Ancient Genealogical Records Prove King David's Descendants are Alive Today," *Breaking Israel News*, August 16, 2016, accessed June 18, 2017, https://www.breakingisraelnews.com/74034/king-davids-descendants-ready-rebuild-davidic-kingdom-jerusalem/#rrrymqrVMD3I5BL6.97. "Honoring King David's Genealogy and Heritage on Behalf of the Jewish People and His Descendants," Davidic Dynasty, accessed June 18, 2017, http://www.davidicdynasty.org/#.

> Now these are those who came up from Tel-melah, Tel-harsha, Cherub, Addan *and* Immer, but **they were not able to give evidence of their fathers' households and their descendants, whether they were of Israel**: the sons of Delaiah, the sons of Tobiah, the sons of Nekoda, 652.
> Of the sons of the priests: the sons of Habaiah, the sons of Hakkoz, **the sons of Barzillai, who took a wife from the daughters of Barzillai the Gileadite**, and he was called by their name. These searched *among* their ancestral registration, but they could not be located; therefore they were considered unclean *and excluded* from the priesthood. **The governor said to them that they should not eat from the most holy things until a priest stood up with Urim and Thummim.** (Ezra 2:59-63, emphasis added; see also Nehemiah 7:61-65)

This is the place where we see the intersection of "physical Israel" and "spiritual Israel"; the mysterious and miraculous interaction of faith and verifiable fact. The Israelites mentioned here are of the House of Judah, but the precedent has bearing on the exiles who will return from the House of Israel.

The list above specifies two groups of people: one from among the common people of Judah, and another from the Levitical priesthood. Both groups maintained their identity, but lacked credible genealogical evidence to verify their claims. Without such evidence, the leaders of the day could have excluded these exiles from the congregation of Israel, leaving them without hope of participating in the blessings and responsibilities of the Covenant. Thus cut off from their people and their heritage, these families would be condemned to be assimilated among the nations.

Such a fate would be especially bitter for the Levites. The very essence of their identity revolved around their God-given purpose as servants of YHVH trusted with the ministry of his holy things. No doubt their family traditions included stirring accounts of their ancestors' service in the Temple courts. Moreover, the Levitical priests mentioned here were descendants of Barzillai, a man who had aided King David when he fled from Absalom, and whom David had directed his son Solomon to honor (2 Samuel 17:26-29,

19:31-39; 1 Kings 2:7). Their grandparents had gone into exile mindful of what they had lost – a memory expressed in a moving psalm:

> By the rivers of Babylon,
> There we sat down and wept,
> When we remembered Zion.
> Upon the willows in the midst of it
> We hung our harps.
> For there our captors demanded of us songs,
> And our tormentors mirth, *saying*,
> "Sing us one of the songs of Zion."
>
> (Psalm 137:1-3)

For 70 years in Babylon, these priestly families looked with eager anticipation to the day they could return home and take up once again their duties. This time they would do it right, teaching the people the difference between the holy and the common so they could avoid the mistakes that had caused the judgment of exile.

Then they hear a devastating word: Judah's leaders had discovered irregularities in their claims of priestly heritage. Problems had arisen in their genealogical records – gaps here and there, and dubious sources of questionable value. Even if they could be considered Israelites (also questionable), they certainly could not be readmitted to the priesthood. Such a decision would condemn these families to a place forever outside the camp, where their names would be cut off from Israel and they would be assimilated among the nations.

And yet, in an Old Testament example of grace, the decision was not final. We do not hear any more about these priestly families, or about the sons of Delaiah, Tobiah,[3] and Nekoda whose very

---

[3] These sons of Tobiah had no relation to Tobiah the Ammonite, one of the opponents of Nehemiah's efforts to rebuild Jerusalem's wall (Nehemiah 2:10, 19). They returned from exile in 537 BCE; the contention with Tobiah the Ammonite occurred over a century later (c. 433 BCE). "Books of Ezra and Nehemiah," Jewish Virtual Library, accessed June 18, 2017, http://www.jewishvirtuallibrary.org/ezra-and-nehemiah-books-of. Peter Enns, "Ezra and Nehemia," The Center for Biblical Studies, accessed June 18, 2017, http://thecenterforbiblicalstudies.org/resources/introductions-to-the-books-of-

identity as Israelites was called into question. However, the nation had taken extreme efforts centuries earlier to preserve the entire seed of Abraham (see Judges 21). Since Scripture does not say otherwise, we conclude that there was a happy ending: either God provided confirmation through priestly verification of their claims, or, despite the lack of physical evidence, the personal and corporate acts of faith regarding their identity kept them from being cut off from the nation.

These families and their brethren of Judah acted in faith: they believed that YHVH would leave a physical remnant to Abraham, and they believed these people were part of that physical remnant. This act of faith brought the solution to the problem: accept the people as Hebrews and include them in the life of the nation, expecting that one day God would confirm their identity.

This precedent addresses a crucial Jewish expectation about the House of Ephraim: they expect a return of physical descendants of the Lost Tribes. As we have seen, this is the basis of Jewish searches over the centuries for the Lost Tribes. Even today it is the expectation that motivates organizations like Shavei Israel.[4] For that reason, prevailing Jewish opinion is disinclined to accept any claims of Israelite identity that do not have basis in physical descent from Abraham, Isaac, and Jacob. In a sense, this contemporary Jewish opinion echoes the attitude John the Baptist encountered in the first century:

> But when he saw many of the Pharisees and Sadducees coming for baptism, he said to them, "You brood of vipers, who warned you to flee from the wrath to come? Therefore bear fruit in keeping with repentance; **and do not suppose that you can say to yourselves, 'We have Abraham for our father'; for I say to you that from these stones God is able to raise up children to Abraham.** (Matthew 3:7-9, emphasis added)

---

the-bible/ezra-and-nehemiah/.

[4] See, for example, the work of Shavei Israel with the Bnei Menashe, one of several people groups in India who claim descent from the Lost Tribes. "Bnei Menashe," Shavei Israel, accessed July 12, 2017, https://shavei.org/communities/bnei-menashe/

A traditional Christian interpretation of this passage is that the Jewish leaders of the day pointed to their lineage as descendants of Abraham as proof of their membership in God's Covenant Nation. Thus, the notion that Israel consisted entirely of Jewish people was alive and well even in the time of Yeshua. As circumcised sons of Abraham, they expected to escape the judgment that would come on the world. Anyone who wanted to escape that judgment would have to become children of Abraham by coming into the nation of Israel through the conversion process and becoming circumcised as Jews. Hence the reason for the expectation – and insistence – that the descendants of the Lost Tribes would have to become Jewish to be grafted back into the nation.

### Raising Up Abraham's Stone-Dead Children

As we have seen, the Apostles thought differently. They shared the prevailing Jewish idea that the entire nation would be restored, with inclusion of those Lost Tribes from the House of Joseph. However, they did not expect them to be Jewish or to become Jewish. The pronouncement by Yeshua's cousin, John the Baptist, speaks to the apostolic expectation. God could, and would, raise up children to Abraham from the very stones.

But how? No Jewish authority, either in the first century or today, would accept claims based on the Christian understanding of salvation by grace through faith in Messiah Yeshua. And yet that is precisely what the Apostles taught.

This presents another dilemma in the division of the Two Houses. It is true that Israel consists of both physical and spiritual components, but they are not separate. Judaism has emphasized the physical component: actual genealogical lineage traced to Abraham, or completion of a rigorous process of conversion to Judaism. Christianity has emphasized the spiritual component: a new Israel distinct from the old physical kingdom, but retaining the same name because Messiah, Son of David, is its king. Each part of the Kingdom defines itself in opposition to the other part. Judaism cannot admit followers of Yeshua because they cannot trace their lineage to Abraham, and because Yeshua himself is perceived as an apostate. Christianity sees the Jewish people as excluded from salvation until they acknowledge Yeshua as Messiah, and believes that the church in its various manifestations is the "Israel of God."[5]

It seems there is no reconciliation of these two positions. But what if both are right? What if Israel by its very definition really is a physical entity, the seed of Abraham passed through Isaac, Jacob, and their descendants across the ages? And, what if inclusion in this Covenant Nation of Abraham's seed really does require an act of faith ratified by the grace of God?

I am persuaded that this is the case.

When YHVH promised Abraham that his descendants would be as numerous as the stars of heaven and the sand of the sea shore (Genesis 15:5, 22:17, 26:4), he meant physical descendants. Moses attested to this in his last address to the people of Israel:

> The LORD your God has multiplied you, and behold, you are this day like the stars of heaven in number. May the LORD, the God of your fathers, increase you a thousand-fold more than you are and bless you, just as He has promised you! (Deuteronomy 1:10-11)

Notice that Moses indicated not only that Abraham's descendants had multiplied as promised in the 470 years since God spoke to the Patriarch, but prayed that they would increase a thousand times more. If there were two to three million people listening to Moses on that day, then he was praying for an Israelite population of two to three *billion*!

---

[5] The case here stated is of necessity a generalization. There are complicated exceptions, such as Messianic Jews who retain their Jewish identity, and who embrace Yeshua as Messiah. While I regard Messianic Jews as fully Jewish and as members of the nation of Israel, mainstream Judaism has a different opinion. Then there are the millions of Anusim now awakening to their Jewish identity after centuries of hiding it. Are they Jewish, and thus members of the nation of Israel, or must they undergo a conversion process? The answers to these questions are beyond the scope of this book. The questions were not resolved in the first century, but we can hope that they will be resolved in our day.

Are there that many Israelites on earth today? Many believe so. The problem is, very few, if any, can trace their lineage back to ancient Israel.

In fact, the only ones who can with any degree of credibility trace their physical descent to Abraham are the Jewish people, and particularly those descendants of the Levitical priesthood and of King David. Everyone else, meaning the House of Joseph, has no hope of proving their lineage. All hope of that vanished over two millennia ago, when the Assyrian Empire completely destroyed Israel's Northern Kingdom.

Thus it would seem that the promise of physical seed from all the tribes has no hope of fulfillment. Except that the hope persists even after 27 centuries of exile. It exists in the people groups who demonstrate Hebraic cultural traits, or with a cultural memory of connection to Israel. These groups exist all over the world, and they number in the hundreds of millions. They include the Bnei Menashe and Bnei Ephraim of India; the Pashtun of Afghanistan and Pakistan; the Kurds of Iraq, Syria, Turkey, and Iran; the Lemba and Igbo of Africa; the Mizo of India and Myanmar; the Aboriginal peoples of Australia; and many peoples among the First Nations of the Americas. They also include the peoples of Europe and the British Isles.

Research into linguistic, anthropological, genetic (DNA), historical, and religious evidence has shown migration patterns of the Ephraimite Tribes to the north, east, west, and south, including Northern and Western Europe and the British Isles. During the age of Europe's empires, the Ephraimite elements of the Spanish, British, French, German, Belgian, and Italian nations spread throughout the colonies of the Americas, Africa, Australia, Asia, New Zealand, and the Pacific Islands. It may safely be concluded, therefore, that in the 2,700 years of Ephraim's exile, the physical seed of Israel's tribes has spread to every single nation and people group on earth.

It does seem that God has scattered the seed of his Covenant Nation into the entire earth. Could that be what Yeshua meant when he spoke the Parable of the Sower, explaining that understanding it was the key to understanding all parables (Mark

4:1-20)? If so, then we have arrived at a new level of meaning not only to this parable, but to Yeshua's mission: not merely to offer personal salvation, but to redeem and regather those Lost Tribes of the House of Joseph.

This point can be summarized with another of Yeshua's Kingdom parables:

> He spoke another parable to them, "The kingdom of heaven is like leaven, which a woman took and hid in three pecks of flour until it was all leavened." (Matthew 13:33)

If the physical seed of Abraham really has been dispersed into every tribe, tongue, and nation, then it is not only possible, but probable that every human being can claim some element of Abraham's DNA in their genes. In truth, the leaven of the kingdom of heaven has leavened the entire lump.

What remains, then, is only to acknowledge this physical descent. Perhaps here is the solution to that age-old Christian debate between free will and predestination. God has predestined Israel to be restored as his holy Covenant Nation, and he has predestined that "all Israel will be saved," meaning all twelve tribes. The free will aspect comes in the choice of every human being: decide whether to be part of this covenant kingdom, or remain outside it and cut off from relationship with the Creator.

My conclusion is that Messiah is the key to this. He is the one who is gathering the Lost Sheep of the House of Israel and, by his atoning death and resurrection, made it possible for us to be grafted back into the nation. We are not grafted into the stick of Judah. Neither are we grafted into a new "spiritual Israel" which has no basis in physical reality. Rather, we are grafted into our own House: the House of Joseph/Ephraim.

This is the solution to the dilemma. We can claim physical descent from Abraham, Isaac, and Jacob simply on the laws of probability that their DNA – their seed – has been dispersed into every people group on earth. Like those exiles returning from Babylon, we cannot produce a genealogy to prove our descent, but we can assert this claim by faith in the hope and expectation that God will confirm it in time.

And, like the Apostle Paul, we can walk away from "myths and endless genealogies, which give rise to mere speculation." (1 Timothy 1:4)

## BENJAMIN'S SPECIAL ROLE

> Benjamin is a ravenous wolf; in the morning he devours the prey, and in the evening he divides the spoil. (Genesis 49:27)

> Of Benjamin he said, "May the beloved of the Lord dwell in security by Him, Who shields him all the day, and he dwells between His shoulders." (Deuteronomy 33:12

Scripture is full of stories that are prophetic in nature. Christians are familiar with the seeming uncanny similarities between Joseph's treatment and life experience as compared to the life and experiences of Yeshua. Both were sold for silver, put in a pit, declared dead, and exiled to Egypt. Eventually, Judah recognized Joseph during the time of Jacob's troubles (famine in the land). The Joseph story in Genesis, however, has another level that directly relates to the restoration of the family and the roles of Judah and Benjamin.

After Joseph had been exiled to Egypt, it was about 20 years before he and his brother Judah again crossed paths. Judah did not recognize Joseph, but Joseph knew full well who Judah was. The very interesting component is that Benjamin, Joseph's brother by the same mother (Rachel), *did* recognize Joseph, according to the Book of Jasher. The story both in Jasher and Genesis explicitly relates the interaction among Judah, Joseph and Benjamin.

What role does Benjamin play today? I find it fascinating that the Apostle Paul, whom I believe preached a Two House message, was a Benjamite (Romans 11:1, Philippians 3:2-6). Even more fascinating is that as I have researched and discussed with others in preparation for this book, I have spoken with many Jews, both Messianic and non-Messianic, who understand the story of the Two Houses. Many believe, but cannot prove, that they are of the tribe of Benjamin.

Coincidence? I don't think so. Rather, it is another crumb on the bread trail toward a full understanding of God's prophetic pictures and utterances.

# 11

# FREQUENTLY ASKED QUESTIONS

The Two House concept is a vast topic that has generated many questions from those who are new to it, as well as from those who are not persuaded that it is a valid interpretation of scripture. In this chapter, I briefly address some of the most common questions. I have provided more thorough answers elsewhere in this book.

**WHY DID GOD DIVIDE THE KINGDOM OF ISRAEL?**

While scripture continues to reveal deeper mysteries and greater understanding, it seems clear at this juncture that God's intent in dividing the Kingdom of Israel was to provide two witnesses on the earth, and to accomplish two purposes through the respective Houses. As explained in chapter 4, each House has a particular purpose. The House of Judah has guarded and transmitted Torah through the ages, while providing evidence through their continued existence as a people of God's covenant faithfulness. The House of Israel has carried Yeshua and his message of redemption to the ends of the earth, demonstrating God's great mercy and bringing others into the Kingdom from all the nations into which they have been scattered. A further reason is that by dividing the family, God, like Jacob, could safely bring his people through history and past the adversary into the Promised Land (Genesis 32, 33). Jews and Christians have each suffered tremendous persecution and threats of annihilation, from Caesars and sultans to Enlightenment thinkers and atheistic despots. Satan, the adversary, from time to time has succeeded in muting the voice of one witness or the other, but he has not silenced them altogether. Thus the Two Witnesses of the Almighty have survived to this day, and even now stand on the threshold of the prophesied restoration of all Israel.

## IS TWO HOUSE THEOLOGY ANOTHER VERSION OF REPLACEMENT THEOLOGY?

Absolutely not! The false accusation that Two House Theology is another form of Replacement Theology stems from a lack of understanding of the scriptures and an improper understanding of Two House theology.

As demonstrated in chapter 4, God's own Law demands at least two witnesses to confirm a matter (Deuteronomy 19:15, Matthew 18:16, 2 Corinthians 13:1, 1 Timothy 5:19, Hebrews 10:28). According to 1 Kings 12:24, the dividing of all Israel was *his* plan. I have further demonstrated that he had a purpose in creating the division, that he showed mercy to each House, and that he gave each a particular purpose in the Plan of Redemption. In doing so, he reveals aspects of his own character and his adherence to his own Law.

Where Two House theology makes Judah nervous is in the prospect of a sudden addition of hundreds of thousands, perhaps millions, of people worldwide coming to Torah and desiring to be connected with Judah, just as prophetic scripture promises. As this has begun happening, there are many on both the Jewish and Christian sides who do not understand the fullness of what is occurring, nor do they understand the enormous cultural and theological differences that continue to cause friction and misunderstandings. My counsel, particularly to those coming from Christianity, is to walk humbly and to be patient, allowing the Lord to work out the details.

By way of comparison, 2 Chronicles 13:3 relates that King Jeroboam had 800,000 warriors available to him when he went to war with Rehoboam's son Abijah. About a century later, in the time of Elijah, 1 Kings 19:15-18 reveals that there were at least 7,000 who had not bowed the knee to Baal (1 Kings 19:15-18). Assuming the two sums are numbers of adult males, and that the proportions would not have changed greatly over the years, those loyal to YHVH amounted to less than 1% of the total population of the House of Israel. Most likely those willing to join with Judah, either at the time of the nation's separation, or after Assyria conquered the Northern Kingdom, would have come from that small number. The vast majority of the House of Israel, therefore, went into exile and have never returned.

Here is an interesting thought regarding the numbers of Israelites in the coming Kingdom. God promised Abraham that his descendants would be, "as the stars of the heavens and as the sand which is on the seashore" (Genesis 22:17). Could it be that the House of Judah is "the stars of the heavens," the visible part of Abraham's seed, and Ephraim is "the sand which is on the seashore," the hidden ones? With a current Jewish population of only around 14 million worldwide, Judah hardly qualifies as the vast throng pictured by this and related prophecies.

According to scripture, the numbers of returning Ephraimites will dwarf Judah. Yet scripture clearly teaches that Judah as the Elder brother has the scepter – the leadership role. The jealousy of Ephraim (Isaiah 11:13) has manifested itself over the centuries in various attempts to wrest this scepter from Judah. In effect, to replace Judah as ruler of the nation. It is understandable that this emerging awareness of non-Jewish Israelite identity has been incorrectly viewed as another manifestation of that jealousy. For that reason, we must be careful to walk in grace and humility, clinging to Messiah Yeshua, while the Father takes care of the details involved in healing 3,000 years of sibling rivalry and the untold human suffering resulting from it.

**HAVEN'T THE LOST TRIBES ALREADY RETURNED?**

Scripture testifies that *elements* of the Northern Kingdom fled to Judah after the division and in later years (2 Chronicles 11:13-17, 15:8-10, 30:1-27, 34:8-9, 35:16-19). Presumably this was to demonstrate the grace of God toward his people. Nevertheless, even after the destruction of the Northern Kingdom the vast majority of those who had not been removed by the Assyrians refused to come under the dominion of Judah (2 Chronicles 30:1-11).

As demonstrated in chapter 5, the Jewish sages in the centuries after the destruction of the Second Temple and during the Middle Ages agree with virtually no dissent that not only had the exiles of the House of Israel never come home, but their return was critically connected with the revealing of the Messiah. The Ramban, the greatest sage of his era, said unequivocally that the exiles had not come home, but that they would.

I do not know of any respected theologian in Judaism or Christianity who believes the Two Stick prophecy of Ezekiel 37 has been fulfilled completely. The simple fact, gleaned from the literal reading of the scriptures, is that only now is it even possible that the Lost Tribes can return. Only in the last decade have most of the prophetic requirements begun to be fulfilled, setting the stage for the Torah Awakening among Christians and the growing desire among many to be allowed to live in the Land.

**WHY IS TWO HOUSE THEOLOGY NOT A HERESY?**

How can the plain text of scripture be heresy? As demonstrated from scripture, through direct statements, historical record, parable, and symbolism, the Two House story and theme is woven into nearly every book of the Bible, and is the major, or only, topic covered by some Prophets.

Two House theology may not fit the paradigms in which we were raised, however, when paradigms clash with scripture, it is the paradigms that need changing – not the verifiable scriptural testimony of Two Houses of Israel being reunited in the Promised Land. *God's* plan was to divide the family, and *God's* plan is to reunite the family. By ending the worst family feud in history, he again demonstrates his sovereignty and power!

**ISN'T THE LAW DONE AWAY WITH? OR AT LEAST IT DOESN'T APPLY TO CHRISTIANS?**

To one degree or another, much of Christianity teaches an incorrect understanding that the Law (the Torah) has been done away with or does not apply to Christians. Scripture paints a different picture. While entire books have been written defending this statement (see *Repairing the Breach* by Peter G. Rambo, Sr.), I will focus this brief discussion on four passages.

- In Matthew 5:17-19, Jesus says not only that he *did not* come to abolish the Law, but that not a single letter will disappear from the Law or the Prophets until heaven and earth pass away (the two witnesses invoked by Moses to testify regarding Israel's inability to keep the Law, and God's justice and mercy in forgiving them; see Deuteronomy 4:25-31, 30:19-20, 31:28). If we want to walk as he walked, we will learn what it means to be obedient to God's everlasting word.
- The New Covenant (Jeremiah 31:31-34; Hebrews 8:8-12), as demonstrated, is not with just anyone, but specifically with the House of Israel and the House of Judah. The prophet Jeremiah further tells us in chapter 31 that under the New Covenant, God will write the Torah on our hearts. If the Torah is truly written on our hearts, we will begin to live it out, even the statutes and the ordinances, as Malachi 4:4 tells us.
- The last few verses of Ezekiel 37 tell us exactly what the Messianic age will look like. Paraphrasing, "My Servant David (the Messiah) will teach Torah in the Land and the House of Jacob, both Houses of Israel, will walk in My statutes and keep My ordinances forever. And, I will make an everlasting covenant of Peace with them."
- Right in the middle of Isaiah 2:1-5, in a passage that speaks to the "last days," the prophet tells us "For the law [Torah] will go forth from Zion, And the word of the Lord from Jerusalem." If the Messiah is going to rule from the mountain of the Lord and the Torah will go forth from Zion, how can it be done away with?

Quite simply, scripture *never* says the Law is done away with. We do not keep the Law for salvation, but because of our salvation, we are called to live as our Messiah did. His example was to live according to the Torah.

## DO YOU MEAN ISRAEL IS MORE THAN JUST THE JEWISH PEOPLE?

Yes! It is a common misperception in both Christianity and Judaism that the terms "Israel" and "Jewish people" are synonymous. In fact, this is not true. Judah was one of 13 tribes.[1] The House of Judah, the Southern Kingdom of Israel, was composed primarily of only three tribes.

As previously stated, *all Jews are Israelites, but not all Israelites are Jews*. The Jews today are the direct descendants of the Southern Kingdom, the House of Judah. They are primarily the tribes of Judah and Benjamin, as well as many Levites attached to them. Additionally, Judah included elements of the Northern Kingdom, as well as much of the tribe of Simeon that they had absorbed during the time of the Judges.

The testimony of scripture is that the House of Israel would be scattered and not regathered until the latter days. Interestingly, through the ages some Jews have been assimilated into the nations, losing their identity, but our covenant-faithful God promises to bring them home as well as companions of the House of Israel in the regathering. This explains the verses in the Two Sticks prophecy of Ezekiel 37 that seem to indicate that elements of all 13 tribes will be present as "companions" in each of the sticks of Judah and the stick of Ephraim:

> The word of the LORD came again to me saying, "And you, son of man, take for yourself one stick and write on it, 'For Judah and for the sons of Israel, his companions'; then take another stick and write on it, 'For Joseph, the stick of Ephraim and all the house of Israel, his companions.'" (Ezekiel 37:15-16)

## WHY DON'T WE HEAR ABOUT THIS FROM MAINSTREAM CHRISTIANITY AND/OR JUDAISM?

The God of Abraham, Isaac, and Jacob is amazingly complex. In a beautiful way, he has had his plan worked out from Creation, yet

---

[1] The twelve sons of Jacob all became fathers of tribes. Most fathered one tribe each, but Joseph, who received the double portion blessing of the firstborn, became the father of two tribes: Ephraim and Manasseh (Genesis 48:8-22, 1 Chronicles 5:1-2). That makes a total of 13 tribes, but scripture still refers to the 12 tribes since the priestly tribe of Levi received no territorial allotment of their own in the Promised Land (Numbers 18:20-24).

he has chosen to reveal parts in stages. As we look in scripture, each part is clearly there, prophesied from the beginning, but we are only given eyes to see when the time is right according to his purposes.

Among the House of Israel, scattered and forgetful of their identity, there have always been non-Jews who have kept Torah to varying degrees. There have been Sabbath-keepers in various Christian sects from the beginning up to the 14$^{th}$ Century and beyond, although they have been persistently persecuted by the Catholic Church, and by Protestant denominations after the Reformation! To a lesser degree, there have been those who have kept the Feasts of the Lord (Leviticus 23), and groups who have eaten only clean foods (Leviticus 11) throughout Christian history, receiving similar marginalization, if not outright persecution. The vast majority, however, have largely continued in the Roman doctrines of church-instituted holidays and separation from Jews.

Much of the salty history of the Christian church and her persecution against any who did not conform to her doctrines, including (and especially) the Jewish people, is a direct result of blindness the Father placed on all of us while he accomplishes his purposes according to his timing. In the midst of this twisted family feud that has lasted for millennia, God has preserved his people, both of Judah and of Israel, and has guided each to fulfill the role he has for them.

Now, at this critical juncture in history, we are blessed to live in a time wherein God is revealing more, though it has always been clearly written in his Word. He is opening the eyes of his people around the world to things in his Word that are necessary for our understanding as we prepare for the next step in the process of redemption.

## Isn't the Church "Spiritual Israel," and aren't the Jews "Physical Israel"?

The Christian church has long had a habit of spiritualizing prophecy that it found difficult to believe could be fulfilled literally. This is a reasonable excuse for the prophetic expectations of Reformers 500 years ago, when there was no meaningful way to imagine a restored nation of Israel and a return of the Jews to the Land. Today, we have no such excuse.

All prophetic scripture that has been fulfilled has always been fulfilled in a very literal way. Often we need hindsight to see it clearly, but scripture is remarkably clear concerning the future of Israel and Judah, and they are clearly prophesied to be in a physical Land with a physical King and a physical Temple. Further, prophecy clearly speaks of a physical regathering, return, and restoration of all the tribes of Israel from both Houses.

As Ezekiel 37:22 prophesies, expect two kingdoms to be brought together by God to reveal his people, the whole House of Jacob – the "one new man" according to Paul in Ephesians 2:15.

## WHERE DOES THE RAPTURE FIT IN ALL OF THIS?

The Rapture is really quite a new doctrine in the growth and development of theological thought over the last two centuries. It is generally based on the idea that at some point the Messiah will appear and take all those who place their faith in him to some other place (heaven?) while he judges the earth and all those upon it. A major passage used to create the scenario comes from Matthew 24 where Yeshua says,

> But immediately after the tribulation of those days the sun will be darkened, and the moon will not give its light, and the stars will fall from the sky, and the powers of the heavens will be shaken. And then the sign of the Son of Man will appear in the sky, and then all the tribes of the earth will mourn, and they will see the Son of Man coming on the clouds of the sky with power and great glory. And He will send forth His angels with a great trumpet and **they will gather together His elect from the four winds, from one end of the sky to the other.** (Matthew 4:29-31, emphasis added)

When we read the Apostolic Writings without taking into account the foundation already established by the Torah and the Prophets, we can be led to wrong interpretations. Yeshua here is making a direct reference to a passage in Deuteronomy 30, where contextually Moses is spelling out the fate of Israel in the latter days. Moses says:

> So it shall be when all of these things have come upon you, the blessing and the curse which I have set before you, and you call *them* to mind in all nations where the Lord your God has banished you, and you return to the Lord your God and obey Him with all your heart and soul according to all that I command you today, you and your sons, then the Lord your God will restore you from captivity, and have compassion on you, and will gather you again from all the peoples where the Lord your God has scattered you. **If your outcasts are at the ends of the earth [Hebrew: "sky"], from there the Lord your God will gather you, and from there He will bring you back.** The Lord your God will bring you into the land which your fathers possessed, and you shall possess it; and He will prosper you and multiply you more than your fathers. (Deuteronomy 30:1-5, emphasis added)

Yeshua is connecting the return of the exiles with his return. Connecting the two passages radically alters the Rapture doctrine from being snatched away to some ethereal location, to being gathered, as all of the Prophets alluded to or stated pointedly, to the Land of Israel to live in the Messiah's Kingdom. Notice that this gathering, as all of the Prophets teach, is contingent upon our obedience and returning, with all of our heart, to the ways of the Father as given to Moses.

**WHERE DOES JESUS/YESHUA FIT IN TWO HOUSE THEOLOGY?**

Simply put, the Two Houses was his plan from the beginning.

Christianity has long focused on one aspect of Yeshua's ministry: that of personal salvation. While this is an important piece of the whole, his ministry was more than that. Demonstrating their clear understanding of the Messiah's role, the disciples' final question of him in Acts 1:6 is, "Lord, is it at this time You are going to restore the Kingdom of Israel?"

Conversely, Judaism's focus has been so much on corporate (national) salvation, a clear mark of the Messiah's prophesied role, that they have not really seen the personal aspect of the Messiah's purpose. This reveals again that the two Houses each have part of the picture, but need each other to display fully the plan and purposes of God and his Messiah.

Yeshua's purpose at his first coming was to make a way for the Lost Sheep of the House of Israel to be grafted back into the Covenant. This is "personal salvation." His purpose at his second coming will be to regather those Lost Sheep and everyone attached to them (meaning all those who are "grafted into" Israel through their faith in Messiah and his redemptive work) from the four corners of the sky (Deuteronomy 30:4; Matthew 24:31), bring them to the Land, and restore the Kingdom over which he will rule and reign.

Therefore, from prophecy we see not only that the Two Houses are instruments of God's plan, but that Yeshua is a key player in accomplishing God's Kingdom purposes.

### ARE YOU SAYING THAT CHRISTIANITY IS ALL WRONG?

Christianity has much that is right and good in it.

There is no denying that great harm has been done in the name of Jesus, a fact that many in the church now recognize and are taking active steps to correct.[2] Nor can anyone deny that Christian practice in each denomination has elements that differ from what is written in the Bible. It is incorrect, however, to point to these shortcomings as proof that Christianity is fundamentally wrong.

---

[2] Repentance for wrongs done in the past is something many Christians worldwide seek to do. This includes repentance to the Jewish people for the sins of omission and commission during the *Shoa* (Holocaust). One organization taking a leading role in this is March of Life (http://www.marchoflife.org), a movement initiated by German pastors Jobst and Charlotte Bittner to organize memorial and reconciliation marches at Holocaust sites all over Europe. March of Life and similar organizations, such as its American counterpart March of Remembrance (http://www.marchofremembrance.org/), are but one part of a global awakening of Christians to break down walls and heal wounds inflicted over the centuries.

Two thousand years of Christian history testify to the *essential rightness* of the Christian message. I could point to the humanitarian work done all over the world by Christians of every sect as evidence that the church has always attempted to live out the commandment to love one's neighbor as one self. This is coupled with a genuine concern for bringing the message of redemption to a world desperately in need of it. I would not have a relationship with the Almighty had it not been for my Christian upbringing, and in that sense I am intimately connected with multitudes of Christians from every tribe and tongue and nation.

What I am saying is that the church is missing something very important. In that sense, I am saying the same thing that reformers over the ages have said. In the days of the Reformation, the missing element was salvation by grace. In the Pentecostal awakening, it was the ministry of the Holy Spirit. In the Torah Awakening, it is the understanding of how Law and Grace work together.

I tis evident that true followers of Jesus already practice most of the Torah. Yeshua said the weightier provisions of the Law are justice, mercy, and faithfulness (Matthew 23:23; see also Micah 6:8 and Deuteronomy 10:12-13). He also identified the two greatest commandments as loving God and loving others (Mark 12:28-31; see also Deuteronomy 6:4-5 and Leviticus 19:18) – the two commandments at the heart of everything written in the Law and the Prophets (Matthew 22:34-40).

What Christians generally do not do is keep Sabbath on the seventh day (Saturday), celebrate the Feasts of the Lord (Passover, Pentecost, Tabernacles, etc.), eat a biblically clean diet per Leviticus 11, or wear *tzitzit* (tassles) on their garments to remind them of God's commandments (Numbers 15:37-41). These are the major provisions of Torah which Jews and Messianic/Hebraic followers of Yeshua honor, but which most of Christianity does not. These are issues the Torah Awakening is bringing to the attention of the church. Like all moves of God, the Torah Awakening is not an end in itself, but a step along the path of his Kingdom restoration.

My premise is that Christianity and Judaism are the Two Witnesses of the Almighty. Neither of them are perfect; each have their errors and blind spots, and yet God has accomplished his purposes through each of them. If our premise is correct, then these Two Witnesses will find new ways to cooperate with one another in mutual respect as they recognize the indispensable role each plays in the prophesied restoration of the Covenant Nation of Israel.

**WHY DON'T YOU CONVERT TO JUDAISM?**

There are two basic reasons why conversion to Judaism is not an option.

First, conversion to Judaism requires denying Yeshua, my Messiah. I cannot do this under any circumstances. Yeshua is the one who brought me into the Covenant, made it possible to become Hebrew, and taught me Torah. Moreover, he did this at the cost of his life, which his heavenly Father restored to him in the resurrection. Denying my Messiah for the short-term goal of being accepted into Israel according to the current criteria of mainstream Judaism and the State of Israel is not worth what I will lose. I expect God himself will bring me and all fellow Ephraimites into full membership in the nation in his time. Until then, we would rather remain in exile with our Messiah than go into the Promised Land without him.

This, by the way, is the main point behind Paul's letter to the Galatians. Non-Jewish followers of Yeshua in the region of Galatia were converting to Judaism in the hope of being accepted into the nation. If, as I have come to understand, the Apostles were teaching that those who came to faith in Yeshua were the returning exiles of Ephraim, along with their companions from all the other nations, then there would have been an expectation among them that they would one day be able to settle in the Promised Land alongside their Jewish compatriots. However, it appears that then, just as now, the outlook of mainstream Judaism was that no one could come into the nation except by becoming Jewish. In other words, undergoing the process called *circumcision*, which involved not only the surgical procedure of circumcision, but the other requirements of coming under rabbinic authority and presenting sacrificial offerings at the Temple.[3] There is no Temple at present, but the elaborate, lengthy, and expensive process of conversion is still the prescribed norm for becoming part of Israel – or at least part of the Jewish portion of Israel. There is faith involved here, but it is not faith in a divine Messiah who has provided atonement to deal with the rebellious heart attitudes that caused our separation in the first place. That is why the apostle wrote:

> Behold I, Paul, say to you that if you receive circumcision, Christ will be of no benefit to you. And I testify again to every man who receives circumcision, that he is under obligation to keep the whole Law. You have been severed from Christ, you who are seeking to be justified by law; you have fallen from grace. For we through the Spirit, by faith, are waiting for the hope of righteousness. For in Christ Jesus neither circumcision nor uncircumcision means anything, but faith working through love. (Galatians 5:2-6)

In brief, undergoing conversion (or "circumcision") means not only saying I have no need of Messiah's redemptive work, but also "switching sticks" – becoming part of the House of Judah. And that leads to the second reason I cannot convert –

Israel is incomplete, and has been ever since the non-Jewish Hebrews of the House of Ephraim left nearly 3,000 years ago. If Ephraimites convert to Judaism, then the nation remains incomplete and God does not fulfill his promises. That is why Paul wrote:

> Only, as the Lord has assigned to each one, as God has called each, in this manner let him walk. And so I direct in all the churches. Was any man called *when he was already* circumcised? He is not to become uncircumcised. Has anyone been called in uncircumcision? He is not to be circumcised. Circumcision is nothing, and uncircumcision is nothing, but *what matters is* the keeping of the

---

[3] John Kimball McKee, "Introduction," in *Galatians for the Practical Messianic* (Richardson, TX: TNN Press, 2012), Kindle.

commandments of God. Each man must remain in that condition in which he was called. (1 Corinthians 7:17-20)

Since "circumcision" in this first-century context means being Jewish or converting to Judaism, then Paul is saying those who came into the Kingdom as Jews should remain Jewish, and those who were Gentiles before coming into the Kingdom should not become Jews. Therefore, I will heed the Apostle's counsel and remain just as I am.

Without the Jewish people, there can be no Israel. Without the Hebrews of Ephraim, Israel cannot be complete.

# THE TRIBES AND THE THRONE OF GOD

In Numbers 2, Moses explains how the tribes were arranged in camps around the Tabernacle. The camp of Judah (Judah, Issachar, Zebulun) was on the east, Reuben (Reuben, Simeon, Gad) on the south, Ephraim (Ephraim, Manasseh, Benjamin) on the west, and Dan (Dan Asher, Naphtali) on the north. When the nation moved, Judah led the way, followed by the camps of Reuben, Ephraim, and Dan. Levites carrying the Tabernacle marched behind Judah, and other Levites carrying the holy objects followed Ephraim.

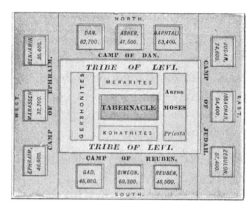

Hurlbut, *Bible Atlas*, 47.

Paul says that natural elements illustrate spiritual truth, and that Israel's wilderness trials are lessons for us (1 Corinthians 10:1-13, 15:46). What, then, do we see in this arrangement of the camp?

Nothing less than a picture of God's glorious throne.

Ezekiel, John, and Jewish tradition help with this. In Ezekiel 1, the prophet sees a vision of God enthroned on the cherubim. He describes the cherubim as living creatures with four faces: that of a man, a lion, a bull (or ox), and an eagle. Compare this to John's vision of the throne room in heaven, where he sees four living creatures with the same faces (Revelation 4:7).

The connection with Israel's camp is in the banners of the tribes (Numbers 2:2). Tradition associates the symbols of a lion with Judah and an ox, bull, or calf with Joseph (both Ephraim and Manasseh) (Genesis 49:8, Deuteronomy 33:17). Reuben, as Jacob's firstborn, often carries the symbol of a man (Reuben means "see, a son"). That leaves the eagle to represent the camp of Dan. There is no scripture to make that direct connection, but the Bible often associates eagles with judgment (Deuteronomy 28:49, Job 9:26, Proverbs 30:17, Jerermiah 4:13, 48:40, 49:22, Lamentations 4:19, Ezekiel 17:3; Hosea 8:1; Habakkuk 1:8, Matthew 24:28; Luke 17:37). Perhaps the link to the eagle is in Jacob's prophecy that Dan is to judge his brothers (Genesis 49:16-18).

When we consider this picture, one lesson we take away is something Jewish sages have known for centuries: that the world will not see the full glory of the Almighty until all the nation is complete, with all the tribes restored to the Promised Land.

# 12

# IMPLICATIONS AND CONCLUSIONS

Nicolaus Copernicus, an astronomer who lived in the early 1500s, had a dilemma. His observable data did not fit the long-established model of the solar system articulated by Ptolemy and endorsed by the Catholic Church. For nearly 1300 years, the prevailing explanation of the solar system, and the universe for that matter, was that everything revolved around the earth. It was the position endorsed and protected by the church that the earth, and therefore man and the church, were at the center of everything.

Copernicus, a Catholic priest as well as an astronomer, was barely 30 years old when he began to notice that the observable data in the heavens did not fit the entrenched astronomic model. Quietly, he began to research, and about the year 1514 began circulating an outline for an alternate theory that answered perplexing problems like the retrograde motion of the planets. In his theory, the earth was *not* the center of the solar system as the Ptolemaic Geocentric model professed. Rather, at the center was Helios, the sun! The planetary system was *heliocentric.* Now Copernicus had a real dilemma. He was at odds with the church and established doctrines. Speaking out could well lead to excommunication, persecution and even death.

Rather than buck the system, he chose to hold his tongue and continue gathering data while quietly teaching the theory to his physics and astronomy students. Maybe the fact that he only taught it as a theory protected him from the strong arm of the church, but just before his death in 1543, he published his research, *De revolutionibus orbium coelestium* (*On the Revolutions of the Celestial Spheres*). It created quite a stir.

Giordano Bruno took up the Copernican model as fact, becoming the first to assert that the stars were actually other suns. He was ultimately tried for heresy by the church for his astronomical and theological beliefs and, on February 17, 1600, was burned at the stake.

Contemporary to Bruno, Johannes Kepler proved Copernicus' theories with much refined mathematic predictions, but paid a heavy price in the loss of professorial positions and excommunication from the Lutheran Church. Apparently, Martin Luther's rant against Copernicus *before the theory had even been published* was sufficient for Lutheran authorities to attempt to destroy Kepler.

Galileo Galilei made out only a little better. Tried for heresy and threatened with execution by the Inquisition, Galileo recanted and agreed to withdraw his books from publication and state that heliocentrism was only a theory. He was not excommunicated, but remained under house arrest until his death.

Today, every kindergartener knows this well-established and unquestioned fact: the earth revolves around the sun. As the historical record shows, though, it was at one point a heretical proposition that ended in execution for some early adherents.

Copernicus was not the first to propose such a revolutionary theory that answered previously unanswerable questions. He was just the first in more than 1500 years. The Greeks had a similar theory, one with which he was largely unfamiliar until late in his research.

Like Copernicus in his study of astronomy, I in my study of the Bible have found perplexing scriptures that do not logically fit the theological paradigms in which I was raised. Unlike most of those around me, I was not satisfied simply to accept answers that didn't make sense. There had to be a better solution, so I set out to find answers. Once I had formed a working theory of how then Scriptures better fit together, I discovered that others had also come to this similar solution: there are Two Houses of Israel in God's plan!

Two House theology, much like Copernicus' heliocentric theory, answers many questions and correctly interprets many prophecies, but it also completely shifts established church doctrine, removing the church from the center of the theological universe. In astronomy, the solar system revolves around the sun, not the earth; *in theology all scripture revolves around Israel, not the church.*

This is a paradigm-shifting assertion. The implications are staggering, and yet they answer previously unanswerable questions. As with others, in my process of making this shift, I have seen many previously unrecognized connections in scripture come suddenly into sharp focus.

Two House theology changes everything, and for the better. All scripture fits together and makes sense, especially the Prophets. Two House theology refined our view and understanding of who we are as followers of Messiah. It changes our view and understanding of the Messiah and his role, it alters radically our perspective of the Jewish people, it adjusts and rightly assembles prophecy, and it dramatically changes our view of the Torah.

**Who We Are as a People**

Christians understand that they are a people and a holy nation, but because we have had no clear understanding of how we are connected with Israel, we have been left to spiritualize and further draw lines of distinction and separation between ourselves and our brethren in the House of Judah. This division has served for two millennia as a breeding ground for strife, envy and jealousy – exactly as scripture prophesied!

Because Christians did not understand how we are a *portion* of Israel, we assumed we were the whole of Israel, and therefore viewed the Jewish people as claiming something that somehow no longer belonged to them. This view has prevailed regardless of the fact that scripture *never* says that the Jewish people were cut out of the Covenant, and contains a myriad of promises clearly pointing to their restoration and return. The existence of the modern State of Israel is living proof of those promises.

Now, understanding the respective roles of the Two Houses and how we fit into YHVH's grand plan, we see that he has given us a place and he will make room for us. We no longer need to compete with or try to usurp Judah's place. With this corrected understanding of our identity, not only can we perform well our role in the nation, we can at last appreciate and support our brother who has a different role in the Divine plan.

The Two House understanding has clarified our identity and eliminated our identity crisis of who we are and how we fit.

**The Role of the Messiah**

In Christianity, we assume the Messiah's primary role is to be a personal savior. While this is a very important aspect of who he is, we have come to realize that it is not his sole or even primary role. He is the King of Israel, and therefore must fulfill the corporate redemptive role of the firstborn. His responsibility is to save and preserve the family, even laying down his life to do so.

Previously, we thought the Messiah would establish some ethereal kingdom in heaven somewhere, and so we glossed over the literal prophecies pointing to a fulfillment here on earth. Yet scripture spells out, over and over, that Messiah will reign over a literal kingdom here on earth, administering justice according to the Torah.

Two House theology clarifies so many questions about Messiah's regathering of Israel, such as –
- what exactly is to happen (an event far greater than the Exodus from Egypt, Jeremiah 16:14-15, 23:7-8),
- who is to be regathered (Judah, Israel, and their companions, Isaiah 56:1-8; Ezekiel 37:15-19),
- why YHVH is doing this (to vindicate his name, Ezekiel 36:16-32),
- when it will happen (after the Time of Jacob's Trouble, Jeremiah 30:4-11; Matthew 24:29-31).

No longer can we think in some twisted way that Yeshua started some new religion and abandoned the everlasting instructions given by YHVH from Mt. Sinai. Rather, we begin to understand that it is when we return to YHVH with all our heart, soul, and mind, and begin to walk in the everlasting Covenant, that the

Messiah will come and regather us to live in the Land of our fathers.

In his Sermon on the Mount, Yeshua was not undermining or altering the Torah. He was plunging beneath the surface of the written word as given to Moses and teaching the heart issues attached to it, exactly as Deuteronomy 18 prophesied he would. Not only did he teach the Torah in fullness, but he lived it as an example for us so that we would know how to do the same. If we walk as he walked, then we will keep the Sabbath and the Feasts of the Lord, and we will eat what God has designated as clean for human consumption.

Two House theology helps us to understand the corporate, or national, aspect of the Messiah's role and his relationship to the whole family. Further, as we understand our place and role in the family, we can correctly focus our work toward the redemption of the world and the good news of the Messiah!

## How We Relate to the Jewish People

As has previously been expounded, the historical relationship between Christians and Jews has not been a good one. At best, it has been strained and untrusting; at worst, it has been tragic and bloody.

A Two House understanding means we are no longer in competition with the Jewish people for YHVH's affection. Rather, we realize that in their particular role of guarding and preserving the Torah, they have much to teach us. Our Jewish brethren bring great riches and giftings to the family table. They have pieces of the whole picture that we do not. We need them as much or more than we think they need us.

Our Jewish brethren are to be honored and respected. And, as hard as this is for some to hear, we do not need to make them into Christians. In the Father's time, *he* will reveal the Messiah to them. All of us *only* come to Yeshua when he is revealed by the Holy Spirit (Deuteronomy 29:29; Daniel 2:20-22; Matthew 11:25, 16:16-17; Galatians 1:13-17; Colossians 3:1-4). None of us come on our own. While we recognize that the Father is awakening some Jews, we must also realize that scripture says their awakening will largely be *en masse* near the end of the age.

> I will pour out on the house of David and on the inhabitants of Jerusalem, the Spirit of grace and of supplication, so that they will look on Me whom they have pierced; and they will mourn for Him, as one mourns for an only son, and they will weep bitterly over Him like the bitter weeping over a firstborn. (Zechariah 12:10)

The greatest blessing we can be to Judah is to support and encourage them to live Torah observant lives and help them as one would help an embattled brother. We can do so by walking before them in peace and humility, supporting the Nation of Israel and her many ministries, as well as by visiting Israel, particularly at the pilgrim feasts (Passover, Pentecost (Shavuot), and Tabernacles). Further, we should build relationships with our Jewish brothers and sisters that are mutually respectful and open to allow dialogue and trust to blossom. Our greatest testimony to the person and work of Yeshua is not handing out tracts, but obediently living like our Messiah by loving our brother, and keeping the Torah.

Two House theology should help us understand and walk out our calling as a brother, even a Prodigal brother, who returns in humility, looking to the Father to open the way for repairing family relationships. Let us simply seek to be good servants in the House of Jacob.

## Prophecy unraveled and clarified

Prophecy can be quite perplexing, particularly when our starting point or paradigm is skewed. Christianity has long been aware of many prophesies that had a physical sounding element to their fulfillment, but because our paradigm did not allow us truly to see ourselves as a *portion* of Israel, we had to marginalize or ignore prophecy we could not explain away.

This lack of understanding, coupled with spiritual pride, caused us to treat the church as if it were a separate entity. That notion disregards Stephen's clear message in Acts 7:38 that the church (Greek – *ekklesia*, Hebrew – *qahal*) was at Mt. Sinai in the Wilderness – as well as the assertion of Hebrews 3:16-4:2 that the same good news of the gospel preached to the congregation at Sinai was what the Apostles preached. If that is true, and it is, then we must understand who we are and how our disobedience at Sinai and afterward led to our exile and eventual promised regathering by the Messiah! All prophecy begins to fit together very nicely without the necessity of ignoring any pieces, or making excuses for why "that doesn't apply anymore."

A proper Two House understanding answers many questions and unlocks so many verses that previously were riddles. Prophecy is no longer a mystery, but a roadmap!

**Rightly Understanding the Torah**

If Two House Theology is correct, then we should begin to understand our very literal connection to the nation of Israel. As part of Israel, we are therefore subject to the everlasting and unchanging Covenant God made at Mt. Sinai. This is perhaps the most challenging leap for most. Christianity has minimized and marginalized Torah into irrelevance, yet nothing could be further from the truth.

As has been stated, whole books have been written concerning our responsibility before God to be obedient to his everlasting and unchanging standards of righteousness. Most Christian theology that seeks to avoid or disregard the Torah stems from the roots of our division from Judah after the first century. At that time in history, Christianity was trying to define itself apart from and in opposition to Judaism in order to avoid persecution. Emperor Constantine of Rome further fueled the separation by instituting severe penalties, including death, on those whose worship included any elements interpreted to be Jewish.

This brings us to an important conclusion: even in 325 AD it was necessary for the Empire to resort to the sword to prevent non-Jewish believers in Messiah from keeping the Feasts of the Lord or worshipping on the seventh-day Sabbath![1] Today, Christianity regards those things as strange, yet nearly 300 years after Yeshua's ascension to the Father they were not strange. Even then, non-Jewish believers were still so faithful in following Messiah's example of obedience to his Torah that Constantine had to threaten them with death to move the church from Sabbath to Sunday, from Passover to Easter, and from clean meats to pork. In the centuries since then, Christianity has come to regard those things as strange, fulfilling Hosea's prophecy:

> Since Ephraim has multiplied altars for sin, they have become altars of sinning for him. **Though I wrote for him ten thousand *precepts* of My law, they are regarded as a strange thing.** (Hosea 8:11-12, emphasis added)

But today, around the world, millions of believers in Yeshua are awakening to rethink their form of worship and the relevance of the everlasting commandments given at Sinai. Untold numbers are returning to the Feasts of the Lord, deemed by God as "perpetual ordinances throughout your generations" (Leviticus 23:14, 21, 31, 41). Countless home fellowships are springing up as families are rediscovering the blessings of the seventh-day Sabbath.

It may be a surprise to realize that Christianity already keeps about 70-75% of the commands written in the Torah. The traditional Jewish understanding is that the five books of Moses contain 613 commands.[2] Many of these apply only to the priests or Levites, and

---

[1] Joseph Farah, *The Restitution of All Things: Israel, Christians, and the End of the Age* (Washington, DC: WND Books, 2017), 104-105, 123-124; Kevin Knight, ed., "First Council of Nicaea (A.D. 325)," Thomas Slater, "Sunday," *The Catholic Encyclopedia*, Vol. 14. (New York: Robert Appleton Company, 1912), accessed July 24, 2017, http://www.newadvent.org/cathen/14335a.htm; Charles Herbermann and Georg Grupp, "Constantine the Great," *The Catholic Encyclopedia*, Vol 4. (New York: Robert Appleton Company, 1908), accessed July 24, 2017, http://www.newadvent.org/cathen/04295c.htm.

[2] A generally accepted list of all 613 is the one compiled by Rabbi Moses ben Maimon (the Rambam, or Maimonides) in his work, *Mishneh Torah*. *The Babylonian Talmud: Tract Maccoth*, trans. Michael L. Rodkinson (Boston: The Talmud Society, 1918), accessed July 24, 2017, https://archive.org/stream/TheBabylonianTalmudVols1-1--MichaelL.Rodkinson/TheBabylonianTalmud-Book9-Vols.XviiXviii-Tr.ByMichaelL.Rodkinson1918#page/n49/mode/2up; Mendy Hecht, "The 613 Commandments," *Chabad.org*, accessed July 24, 2017, http://www.chabad.org/library/article_cdo/aid/756399/jewish/The-613-

can only be observed if there is a Temple with priests serving in it. Others can be observed only by people living in the Land, and still others apply to specific categories of people, such as farmers and public officials. The average individual is left with about 200 commands that focus on how to love God and love our neighbors. The major marks that Christianity misses can be summed up in three areas: Sabbath, Feasts of the Lord, and God's dietary instructions.

When we understand that the church is not some separate entity, but the House of Israel, part of the Commonwealth along with our brother Judah, then we quickly understand that we have a national constitution: the Torah. In it we find practical, detailed instructions concerning how we are to love God with all of our heart, soul, mind and strength, and love our neighbor as ourselves. These instructions are the same for everyone, just as YHVH declared three times in Torah (Exodus 12:48, Numbers 15:16, 29), and as Paul confirmed in his letter to the disciples of Yeshua in Rome:

> Do we then nullify the Law through faith? May it never be!
> On the contrary, we establish the Law. (Romans 3:31)

With this Two House perspective, we understand why God, in the New Covenant, desires to write the Torah on our hearts! We are his people and the sheep of his pasture! Amazingly, the Tanakh – the "Old Testament" – is suddenly *NEW!* And *PERSONAL!* It is our own history, a record of where we came from, where we have been, where we are today, and why. Moreover, it is the instruction to return to the Covenant and the Land of our fathers.

**Final Thoughts**

So much more could be written on the subject of the two Houses. There are many, many more passages of scripture that support what has been shared in this book, but I trust that through this brief introduction your appetite is sufficiently whetted and your eye

---

Commandments.htm; Tracey R. Rich, "A List of the 613 Mitzvot (Commandments), *Judaism 101*, accessed October 24, 2017, http://www.jewfaq.org/613.htm.

sharpened. I hope you will begin to see more pieces that fit into this grand picture as you realize your identity not only in Messiah but as *a portion* of Israel.

There are those who, for various reasons, will not like these assertions, but none have yet offered a single compelling reason that this Two House perspective is not the correct paradigm for understanding scripture and our place in the Kingdom. I can only hope that detractors will honestly get before the Father to ask if this is indeed the truth.

The lost House of Israel could not return before now. We, the Ephraimites, could not come back 20 centuries ago. For one thing, the dispersion to the ends of the earth and into every nation was not complete, and we had to fulfill the prophesied length of the exile. For another, we might well have been absorbed into Judah. We needed 20 centuries of Christian testimony to prepare us. In that time, God prepared our hearts by revealing himself over and over to us and our fathers and mothers.

Our testimony of Jesus Christ is very real, and no less real because we know him now as Messiah Yeshua. The testimonies of C.S. Lewis, Billy Graham, Martin Luther King, Jr., Lottie Moon, Horatio Spafford, Julia Ward Howe, Fanny Crosby, Richard Allen, James Varick, John Newton, John and Charles Wesley, Cotton Mather, William Penn, the Moravian Brethren, Jan Hus, John Wycliffe, William Tyndale, and multitudes more going all the way to the first generation of believers are solidly real. Heaven and earth have moved on behalf of the Christian church as God spared no effort to seek and to save that which was lost. He had to put the message into a form that the lost sheep could hear and understand and receive. That meant it had to be separate from Judaism.

The Jewish voice, then as now, seeks to reunite the tribes under Judean domination, demanding conversion to Judaism as the price of admission. This exceeds the godly leadership role of the Elder brother who wields the scepter, and recalls the reasons the Ten Tribes rebelled in the first place. But then, the Christian voice has done no differently, seeking to build an Israel devoid of any Jewish voice. Thus the jealousy of Ephraim and the vexation of Judah, as they have played out over the last 20 centuries, have demonstrated the wisdom of the Father in causing us all to develop in our separate relationships with him.

Hopefully by now we know better. In the beginning, Judah introduced us to YHVH, but our relationship with him has developed independently of Judah. And now, the heavenly Father we have come to know is beginning to open our eyes to our forgotten identity as Hebrews. We can at last stand confidently, yet humbly, in our own identity.

It should be no surprise that the catalyst for the Torah Awakening and the subsequent Ephraimite Awakening among Christians is the advent of Messianic Judaism. Just as the first witnesses to Messiah's coming 2,000 years ago were Jewish, the witnesses to the eternal truth of Torah and its applicability to all people have been Jewish. As our identity in Messiah Yeshua has matured as a people, and as prophetic expectations of his imminent return have excited multitudes, the faithful witness of modern Messianic Judaism to the Hebrew Roots of our faith has added a crucial missing element. In a very real way, the Two House message among Hebrew Roots believers is the fruit of the pioneering work of Messianic Jewish teaching, and the cooperation that has arisen between Messianic Judaism and the Christian church. Thus we see in this, as in the pioneering work of Yeshua's Jewish witnesses 2,000 years ago, the beginning of the fulfillment of Zechariah's prophecy:

> Thus says the LORD of hosts, "*It will* yet *be* that peoples will come, even the inhabitants of many cities. The inhabitants of one will go to another, saying, 'Let us go at once to entreat the favor of the LORD, and to seek the LORD of hosts; I will also go.' So many peoples and mighty nations will come to seek the LORD of hosts in Jerusalem and to entreat the favor of the LORD." Thus says the LORD of hosts, **"In those days ten men from all the nations will grasp the garment of a Jew, saying, 'Let us go with you, for we have heard that God is with you.'"** (Zechariah 8:20-23, emphasis added)

We owe a debt of honor and gratitude to Messianic Judaism for sharing the truth of Torah and its relevance to all believers, Jewish and non-Jewish. Even as Benjamin stood between his brothers in ancient Egypt, and as Paul the Benjamite did in the first century, Messianic Judaism stands between the Jewish testimony of the Creator proclaimed by Judah, and the Christian testimony of the Creator's redemption, proclaimed by Joseph. We prayerfully long for the day when our Messianic Jewish brothers fulfill their Benjamin call and role to be the bridge between Joseph and Judah.

Long ages ago, when King David returned from self-imposed exile after the civil war begun by his son Absalom, the Two Houses of Israel nearly came to blows over their identity in the King. The men of Israel were right to say that simple numbers – ten tribes against two – gave them "more *claim* on David" (2 Samuel 19:43) than Judah. Yet the harsh words spoken by the Judeans in their defense were also justified: David was their flesh and blood, and reigned as king over them before he became king over all Israel (2 Samuel 2:11). The controversy has not abated to this day. The descendants of the House of Israel claim allegiance to the King, while the descendants of the House of Judah cling more tightly to the Kingdom. In truth, King and Kingdom are inseparable. When all the children of Jacob realize that and begin working to bring the two sticks of Judah and Joseph closer together, then we will see Messiah Son of David come and make them one people again.

May it be soon and in our day.

*Hazak, hazak, v'nit'chazek!*

# ABOUT THE AUTHOR

**Peter G. Rambo, Sr.**
Pete Rambo is a school bus driver and trainer. He formerly pastored a congregation for 10 years before leading a Messianic congregation and home fellowship. His education includes a BA in Natural Science from Erskine College and a Masters of Divinity from Columbia International University and Biblical Seminary. Since beginning to understand the Hebrew roots of his faith, he has maintained *natsab.com*, a blog dedicated to sharing what he is learning on this journey of discovery. In 2016 he authored *Repairing the Breach*, a collection of articles that provide a strong defense for a Christian's relationship to the Torah and the Messiah. In the same year he was on the founding team and served as Director of Operations for B'ney Yosef North America, an organization dedicated to gathering and encouraging those of the House of Israel in North America. In 2018, along with several visionaries from Europe and the US, he helped found and currently is the Director of Ani Yosef (aniyosef.com), an organization that takes international teams to Israel during the feasts to pick up trash and present ourselves before YHVH. He is married to Kelly and has four sons who help with the small family farm in Newberry, SC.

Made in the USA
Middletown, DE
25 February 2023

25337371R00116